# ARISTOPHANES

## FOUR MAJOR PLAYS

*Lysistrata*
*The Birds*
*The Clouds*
*The Archarnians*

*AIRMONT* BOOKS

**AIRMONT BOOKS**
NEW YORK

THE SPECIAL CONTENTS OF THIS EDITION
ⓒ, Copyright, 1969, by
Airmont Publishing Company, Inc.

ISBN: 0-8049-0189-9

PRINTED IN THE UNITED STATES OF AMERICA

AIRMONT PUBLISHING CO., INC.,   New York, N.Y.

# CONTENTS

# Aristophanes

## FOUR MAJOR PLAYS

## *INTRODUCTION*

After twenty centuries, the comic genius of Aristophanes remains unique. For the great Athenian—like all supreme artists—created his own universe: a universe impervious to time. His subject matter was man and his foibles, in all their ridiculous manifestations. He enumerated, anatomized, and impaled them on a savage blade of uproarious laughter. Reading him today—in our own age of missiles and computers—is to recognize again and again the abiding truth of his scathing, hilarious indictment. Perhaps laughter is still the only antidote to life on this most troubled of planets.

The facts of Aristophanes' personal life are shrouded in even heavier mist than those of Shakespeare's. All is conjecture, gleaned from occasional allusions in his plays. (He produced more than forty, only eleven are extant.) Born about 444 B.C., probably at Athens, he died in 380 B.C. (?). Of his three sons, nothing is known. The central and dominating event in his life was the Peloponnesian War (431–404 B.C.). The rest is silence.

Aristophanes, like Shakespeare, was fortunate in being born at the right time. This simply means that our dramatist's extraordinary gifts and the taste of his audience magically coincided. The great Age of Pericles was gone, but the glow still lingered. Fifth century, B.C., Athens harbored a citizenry whose intellectual curiosity and vitality was exceeded only by their physical vigor and Rabelaisian appetite. The typical Athenian spectator was equally at home with soaring tragedy and side-splitting farce. (In this, he resembled Shakespeare's groundling.) His imaginative receptivity knew no bounds. Nothing human was alien to him. Not even the gods were above reproach. There were no sacred cows.

Through this hurly-burly, seething city stalked Aristophanes: a man whose jaundiced eye encompassed practically every phase of Athenian life—and found each wanting. Current politics and morality were his chief targets. But he had ample room for withering blasts at literary fashions, educational malpractices, bogus economic theories, legal chicanery, and so much more. A conservative by instinct and choice, he spared neither his party nor class. He

5

# INTRODUCTION

longed for the more spacious days of the "Men of Marathon" to whom Athens owed both her freedom and her glory. But they were gone forever. And his rage found release in satiric comedies that claw, rip, and vilify, but above all—entertain.

The comedy of Aristophanes—designated Old Comedy—differs from the Comedy of Manners as practiced by a Menander of later date. It is anything but private or domestic. Nor is it a mere mirror of polite society and its foibles. Technically, Aristophanic comedy includes such elements as burlesque, farce, comic opera, and pantomime. And though the objective is uproarious fun, its basic seriousness of intent is always in evidence. The action of the play is divided into two parts. Francis M. Cornford, in "The Origin of Attic Comedy," describes the first part as follows: "The (first) part normally consists of the *Prologue*, or opposition scenes; the Entrance of the Chorus (*Parados*); and what is now generally called the *Agon*, a fierce "contest" between the representatives of two parties or principles, which are in effect the hero and the villain of the whole piece." Perhaps the most distinctive feature of Old Comedy is the *Parabasis* of the Chorus. Coming midway through the play, this device enables the dramatist, in the persons of the Leaders and the Chorus, to speak directly to the audience. The action of the play is suspended—the actors leave the stage—and the poet ranges over any topic he desires: politics, topical allusions, etc. At the conclusion of the *Parabasis*, the play resumes. Old Comedy employs only three actors and a chorus. The latter usually engaged in the dialogue, and divided the action by song and dance. One note more. To deny the obscenity that abounds in the work of Aristophanes would be tantamount to ignoring the culture that produced it. The rollicking spirit of the Athenian audience and their zest for life permitted no taboos. Their inherent sanity and health enabled them to accept all things human as part of the very nature of life.

*The Acharnians* (426 B.C.) gained first prize at the Lenaean Festival. It was the first play produced by Aristophanes under his name, and marked his emergence as a dramatist to be reckoned with. The theme of the play is the conflict between the Parties of War (Cleon) and Peace (Dicaeopolis). The plot is simple. Dicaeopolis, an Athenian citizen, but a native of Acharnae—an agricultural community devastated by the Lacedaemonian invasions —urges peace at any price. Demagogue Cleon and his henchmen refuse to entertain so heinous a thought. Dicaeopolis, therefore, sues for a personal true with Sparta—to the consternation of the War Party. Negotiations are finally concluded, and the play ends with a riotous feast in honor of Peace and Plenty. Besides Cleon, this play introduces another of Aristophanes' favorite targets—the great dramatist Euripides. However, it is not so much the man and

# INTRODUCTION

his work that Aristophanes inveighs against, but rather the effects of that work upon the taste and morality of the Athenian citizen. Moreover, our poet was always suspicious of language that did not conform to his own ideas of Attic strength and simplicity.

*The Birds* (414 B.C.) is unique among Aristophanic comedy. Its purpose is sheer entertainment—possibly an attempt to ease the audience's tension induced by the Sicilian Expedition. For one, the invective and usual targets are missing. *The Birds* is gossamer fresh, its lyric poetry truly ravishing. Two Athenians, Euelpides and Pisthetaerus, weary of the litigiousness, hypocrisy, and sycophancy rampant in their city, resolve to find a Shangri-la at any price. They journey to the land of Epops, King of the Birds. After sundry mishaps, they finally meet both the King and his followers. Before a multi-colored convocation, they relate their startling plan. Power must be wrested from the gods of Olympus and transferred to the hands—or claws—of the feathered brethren. A new city must be erected—"Cloud-cuckoo-land"—between heaven and earth. It must be controlled and protected by flocks of birds ever alert to intercept communiqués between the gods and their earth-worshippers. It will be a city free from the imbroglios of law courts and politics—a haven of peace and quiet. Amidst thunderous applause, the plan is adopted. The city is built, and the plan succeeds only too well. Prometheus is forced to intercede with Epops on behalf of the gods who are in dire straits. Other emissaries from the Olympians follow. Finally, with the marriage of Pisthetaerus and Basileia—handmaiden of Zeus—all is resolved. The birds win their just demands.

*The Clouds* (423 B.C.) satirizes the intelligentsia and Socrates who "walks on air and contemplates the sun." The ridiculing of so extraordinary a man is explicable only in terms of Aristophanes' principles and passionate prejudices. Our dramatist greatly feared the "new education" of the Sophists. He believed that they and their doctrines were instrumental in enervating the moral fibre of the young and consequently, the very foundations of the state. Aristophanes had neither the time nor inclination for fine discriminations and subtleties. What better way to hammer home his dire warnings than by castigating their ostensible leader? The effect was all; exact truth was inconsequential. Nevertheless, *The Clouds* is vastly entertaining.

Briefly, the play relates the sad saga of Strepsiades, father of a spendthrift son, Phidippides. Besieged by creditors, the beleaguered father enrolls at the "Thinking School" of Socrates. His idealistic purpose is to learn how to avoid paying his debts. Unfortunately, he is not a very apt pupil, and is summarily dismissed. Undaunted, however, he insists on sending his charming son to this school of learning. The results are disastrous. For Phidippides learns his lessons so well that he can now thrash his father while justifying his

# INTRODUCTION

gentle behavior with consummate logic. Strepsiades, now utterly bereft, burns down the "Thinking School."

*Lysistrata* (411 B.C.) is perhaps the best known of Aristophanes' comedies. Certainly, it is the most frequently performed. In it, Aristophanes returns to his favorite theme—war and its attendant evils. (It is now the twenty-first year of the seemingly endless Peloponnesian War.) This time, however, he offers a most novel, burlesque solution—a solution that has intrigued and amused both readers and audiences down through the years.

Hellenic women are in despair. Neglected by their men who pay them cursory visits before rushing off to yet another battle front, they finally decide to take matters in their own fragile hands. Led by Lysistrata, an Athenian woman, they vow never again to cohabit with their husbands until a lasting peace is declared. Their victory is inevitable, and in the process, Aristophanes fashions a play of rich sensuality and coruscating wit.

The comedies of Aristophanes mirror the Greek world in all its complexities. Court-jester, moral crusader, social uplifter, philosopher—these are but some of the roles he played so magnificently. But primarily he was a poet: a man whose bolts of laughter still strike home in the hearts and minds of men.

"The Graces, seeking an imperishable sanctuary, found the soul of Aristophanes." Plato's epitaph for this great Athenian is the verdict of history.

N. R. Teitel
New York University

# LYSISTRATA

# LYSISTRATA

## *Dramatis Personae*

LYSISTRATA.
CALONICÉ.
MYRRHINÉ.
LAMPITO.
STRATYLLIS.
A MAGISTRATE.
CINESIAS.
A CHILD.
HERALD OF THE LACEDAEMONIANS.
ENVOYS OF THE LACEDAEMONIANS.
POLYCHARIDES.
MARKET LOUNGERS.
A SERVANT.
AN ATHENIAN CITIZEN.
CHORUS OF OLD MEN.
CHORUS OF WOMEN.

SCENE: In a public square at Athens; afterwards before the gates of the Acropolis, and finally within the precincts of the citadel.

# LYSISTRATA

*Lysistrata.* Ah! if only they had been invited to a Bácchic revelling, or a feast of Pan or Aphrodité or Genetyllis, why! the streets would have been impassable for the thronging tambourines! Now there's never a woman here—ah! except my neighbour Calonicé, whom I see approaching yonder. . . . Good day, Calonicé.

*Calonicé.* Good day, Lysistrata; but pray, why this dark, forbidding face, my dear? Believe me, you don't look a bit pretty with those black lowering brows.

*Lysistrata.* Oh, Calonicé, my heart is on fire; I blush for our sex. Men *will* have it we are tricky and sly. . . .

*Calonicé.* And they are quite right, upon my word!

*Lysistrata.* Yet, look you, when the women are summoned to meet for a matter of the last importance, they lie abed instead of coming.

*Calonicé.* Oh! they will come, my dear; but 'tis not easy, you know, for women to leave the house. One is busy pottering about her husband; another is getting the servant up; a third is putting her child asleep or washing the brat or feeding it.

*Lysistrata.* But I tell you, the business that calls them here is far and away more urgent.

13

*Calonicé.* And why *do* you summon us, dear Lysistrata? What is it all about?

*Lysistrata.* About a big affair.

*Calonicé.* And is it thick too?

*Lysistrata.* Yes indeed, both big and great.

*Calonicé.* And we are not all on the spot!

*Lysistrata.* Oh! if it were what you suppose, there would be never an absentee. No, no, it concerns a thing I have turned about and about this way and that of many sleepless nights.

*Calonicé.* It must be something mighty fine and subtle for you to have turned it about so!

*Lysistrata.* So fine, it means just this, Greece saved by the women!

*Calonicé.* By women! Why, its salvation hangs on a poor thread then!

*Lysistrata.* Our country's fortunes depend on us—it is with us to undo utterly the Peloponnesians.

*Calonicé.* That would be a noble deed truly!

*Lysistrata.* To exterminate the Boeotians to a man!

*Calonicé.* But surely you would spare the eels.

*Lysistrata.* For Athens' sake I will never threaten so fell a doom; trust me for that. However, if the Boeotian and Peloponnesian women join us, Greece is saved.

*Calonicé.* But how should women perform so wise and glorious an achievement, we women who dwell in the retirement of the household, clad in diaphanous garments of yellow silk and long flowing gowns, decked out with flowers and shod with dainty little slippers?

*Lysistrata.* Nay, but those are the very sheet-anchors of our salvation—those yellow tunics, those scents and slippers, those cosmetics and transparent robes.

*Calonicé.* How so, pray?

*Lysistrata.* There is not a man will wield a lance against another . . .

*Calonicé.* Quick, I will get me a yellow tunic from the dyer's.

*Lysistrata.* . . . or want a shield.

*Calonicé.* I'll run and put on a flowing gown.

*Lysistrata.* . . . or draw a sword.

*Calonicé.* I'll haste and buy a pair of slippers this instant.

*Lysistrata.* Now tell me, would not the women have done best to come?

*Calonicé.* Why, they should have *flown* here!

*Lysistrata.* Ah! my dear, you'll see that like true Athenians, they will do everything too late. . . . Why, there's not a woman come from the shoreward parts, not one from Salamis.

*Calonicé.* But I know for certain they embarked at daybreak.

*Lysistrata.* And the dames from Acharnae! why, I thought they would have been the very first to arrive.

*Calonicé.* Theagenes' wife at any rate is sure to come; she has actually been to consult Hecaté. . . . But look! here are some arrivals—and there are more behind. Ah! ha! now what countrywomen may they be?

*Lysistrata.* They are from Anagyra.

*Calonicé.* Yes! upon my word, 'tis a levy *en masse* of all the female population of Anagyra!

*Myrrhiné.* Are we late, Lysistrata? Tell us, pray; what, not a word?

*Lysistrata.* I cannot say much for you, Myrrhiné! you have not bestirred yourself overmuch for an affair of such urgency.

*Myrrhiné.* I could not find my girdle in the dark. However, if the matter is so pressing, here we are; so speak.

*Lysistrata.* No, but let us wait a moment more, till the women of Boeotia arrive and those from the Peloponnese.

*Myrrhiné.* Yes, that is best. . . . Ah! here comes Lampito.

*Lysistrata.* Good day, Lampito, dear friend from Lacedaemon. How well and handsome you look! what a rosy complexion! and how strong you seem; why, you could strangle a bull surely!

*Lampito.* Yes, indeed, I really think I could. 'Tis because I do gymnastics and practise the kick dance.

*Lysistrata.* And what superb bosoms!

*Lampito.* La! you are feeling me as if I were a beast for sacrifice.

*Lysistrata.* And this young woman, what country-woman is she?

*Lampito.* She is a noble lady from Boeotia.

*Lysistrata.* Ah! my pretty Boeotian friend, you are as blooming as a garden.

*Chorus.* Yes, on my word! and the garden is so prettily weeded too!

*Lysistrata.* And who is this?

*Lampito.* 'Tis an honest woman, by my faith! she comes from Corinth.

*Lysistrata.* Oh! honest, no doubt then—as honesty goes at Corinth.

*Lampito.* But who has called together this council of women, pray?

*Lysistrata.* I have.

*Lampito.* Well then, tell us what you want of us.

*Lysistrata.* With pleasure, my dear.

*Myrrhiné.* What is the most important business you wish to inform us about?

*Lysistrata.* I will tell you. But first answer me one question.

*Myrrhiné.* What is that?

*Lysistrata.* Don't you feel sad and sorry because the fathers of your children are far away from you with the army? For I'll undertake, there is not one of you whose husband is not abroad at this moment.

*Calonicé*. Mine has been the last five months in Thrace
—looking after Eucrates.

*Lysistrata*. 'Tis seven long months since mine left me
for Pylos.

*Lampito*. As for mine, if he ever does return from service, he's no sooner back than he takes down his shield
again and flies back to the wars.

*Lysistrata*. And not so much as the shadow of a lover!
Since the day the Milesians betrayed us, I have never
once seen an eight-inch-long *godemiche* even, to be a
leathern consolation to us poor widows. . . . Now tell
me, if I have discovered a means of ending the War,
will you all second me?

*Myrrhiné*. Yes verily, by all the goddesses, I swear I
will, though I have to put my gown in pawn, and drink
the money the same day.

*Calonicé*. And so will I, though I must be split in two
like a flat-fish, and have half myself removed.

*Lampito*. And I too; why, to secure Peace, I would
climb to the top of Mount Taygetus.

*Lysistrata*. Then I will out with it at last, my mighty
secret! Oh! sister women, if we would compel our husbands to make peace, we must refrain . . .

*Myrrhiné*. Refrain from what? tell us, tell us!

*Lysistrata*. But will you do it?

*Myrrhiné*. We will, we will, though we should die of it.

*Lysistrata*. We must refrain from the male altogether.
. . . Nay, why do you turn your backs on me? Where are
you going? So, you bite your lips, and shake your heads,
eh? Why these pale, sad looks? why these tears? Come,
will you do it—yes or no? Do you hesitate?

*Myrrhiné*. No, I will not do it; let the War go on.

*Lysistrata*. And you, my pretty flat-fish, who declared
just now they might split you in two?

*Calonicé*. Anything, anything but that! Bid me go

through the fire, if you will; but to rob us of the sweetest thing in all the world, my dear, dear Lysistrata!

*Lysistrata.* And you?

*Myrrhiné.* Yes, I agree with the others; I too would sooner go through the fire.

*Lysistrata.* Oh, wanton, vicious sex! the poets have done well to make tragedies upon us; we are good for nothing then but love and lewdness! But you, my dear, you from hardy Sparta, if *you* join me, all may yet be well; help me, second me, I conjure you.

*Lampito.* 'Tis a hard thing, by the two goddesses it is! for a woman to sleep alone without ever a strong male in her bed. But there, Peace must come first.

*Lysistrata.* Oh, my dear, my dearest, best friend, you are the only one deserving the name of woman!

*Calonicé.* But if—which the gods forbid—we do refrain altogether from what you say, should we get peace any sooner?

*Lysistrata.* Of course we should, by the goddesses twain! We need only sit indoors with painted cheeks, and meet our mates lightly clad in transparent gowns of Amorgos silk, and employing all our charms and all our arts; then they will act like mad and they will be wild to lie with us. That will be the time to refuse, and they will hasten to make peace, I am convinced of that!

*Lampito.* Yes, just as Menelaus, when he saw Helen's naked bosom, threw away his sword, they say.

*Calonicé.* But, poor devils, suppose our husbands go away and leave us.

*Lysistrata.* Then, as Pherecrates says, we must "flay a skinned dog," that's all.

*Calonicé.* Bah! these proverbs are all idle talk. . . . But if our husbands drag us by main force into the bedchamber?

*Lysistrata.* Hold on to the door posts.

*Calonicé.* But if they beat us?

*Lysistrata.* Then yield to their wishes, but with a bad grace; there is no pleasure for them, when they do it by force. Besides, there are a thousand ways of tormenting them. Never fear, they'll soon tire of the game; there's no satisfaction for a man, unless the woman shares it.

*Calonicé.* Very well, if you *will* have it so, we agree.

*Lampito.* For ourselves, no doubt we shall persuade our husbands to conclude a fair and honest peace; but there is the Athenian populace, how are we to cure these folk of their warlike frenzy?

*Lysistrata.* Have no fear; we undertake to make our own people hear reason.

*Lampito.* Nay, impossible, so long as they have their trusty ships and the vast treasures stored in the temple of Athené.

*Lysistrata.* Ah! but we have seen to that; this very day the Acropolis will be in our hands. That is the task assigned to the older women; while we are here in council, they are going, under pretence of offering sacrifice, to seize the citadel.

*Lampito.* Well said indeed! so everything is going for the best.

*Lysistrata.* Come, quick, Lampito, and let us bind ourselves by an inviolable oath.

*Lampito.* Recite the terms; we will swear to them.

*Lysistrata.* With pleasure. Where is our Usheress? Now, what are you staring at, pray? Lay this shield on the earth before us, its hollow upwards, and someone bring me the victim's inwards.

*Calonicé.* Lysistrata, say, what oath are we to swear?

*Lysistrata.* What oath? Why, in Aeschylus, they sacrifice a sheep, and swear over a buckler; we will do the same.

*Calonicé.* No, Lysistrata, one cannot swear peace over a buckler, surely.

*Lysistrata.* What other oath do you prefer?

*Calonicé.* Let's take a white horse, and sacrifice it, and swear on its entrails.

*Lysistrata.* But where get a white horse from?

*Calonicé.* Well, what oath shall we take then?

*Lysistrata.* Listen to me. Let's set a great black bowl on the ground; let's sacrifice a skin of Thasian wine into it, and take oath not to add one single drop of water.

*Lampito.* Ah! that's an oath pleases me more than I can say.

*Lysistrata.* Let them bring me a bowl and a skin of wine.

*Calonicé.* Ah! my dears, what a noble big bowl! what a delight 'twill be to empty it!

*Lysistrata.* Set the bowl down on the ground, and lay your hands on the victim. . . . Almighty goddess, Persuasion, and thou, bowl, boon comrade of joy and merriment, receive this our sacrifice, and be propitious to us poor women!

*Calonicé.* Oh! the fine red blood! how well it flows!

*Lampito.* And what a delicious savour, by the goddesses twain!

*Lysistrata.* Now, my dears, let me swear first, if you please.

*Calonicé.* No, by the goddess of love, let us decide that by lot.

*Lysistrata.* Come, then, Lampito, and all of you, put your hands to the bowl; and do you, Calonicé, repeat in the name of all the solemn terms I am going to recite. Then you must all swear, and pledge yourselves by the same promises,—*I will have naught to do whether with lover or husband . . .*

*Calonicé. I will have naught to do whether with lover or husband . . .*

*Lysistrata. Albeit he come to me with strength and passion . . .*

*Calonicé.* Albeit he come to me with strength and passion . . . Oh! Lysistrata, I cannot bear it!

*Lysistrata.* I will live at home in perfect chastity . . .

*Calonicé.* I will live at home in perfect chastity . . .

*Lysistrata.* Beautifully dressed and wearing a saffron-coloured gown . . .

*Calonicé.* Beautifully dressed and wearing a saffron-coloured gown . . .

*Lysistrata.* To the end I may inspire my husband with the most ardent longings.

*Calonicé.* To the end I may inspire my husband with the most ardent longings.

*Lysistrata.* Never will I give myself voluntarily . . .

*Calonicé.* Never will I give myself voluntarily . . .

*Lysistrata.* And if he has me by force . . .

*Calonicé.* And if he has me by force . . .

*Lysistrata.* I will be cold as ice, and never stir a limb . . .

*Calonicé.* I will be cold as ice, and never stir a limb . . .

*Lysistrata.* I will not aid him in any way . . .

*Calonicé.* I will not aid him in any way . . .

*Lysistrata.* Nor will I crouch like carven lions on a knife-handle.

*Calonicé.* Nor will I crouch like carven lions on a knife-handle.

*Lysistrata.* And if I keep my oath, may I be suffered to drink of this wine.

*Calonicé.* And if I keep my oath, may I be suffered to drink of this wine.

*Lysistrata.* But if I break it, let my bowl be filled with water.

*Calonicé.* But if I break it, let my bowl be filled with water.

*Lysistrata.* Will ye all take this oath?

*Myrrhiné.* Yes, yes!

*Lysistrata.* Then lo! I'll now consume this remnant (*She drinks.*)

*Calonicé.* Enough, enough, my dear; now let us all drink in turn to cement our friendship.

*Lampito.* Hark! what do those cries mean?

*Lysistrata.* 'Tis what I was telling you; the women have just occupied the Acropolis. So now, Lampito, do you return to Sparta to organize the plot, while your comrades here remain as hostages. For ourselves, let us away to join the rest in the citadel, and let us push the bolts well home.

*Calonicé.* But don't you think the men will march up against us?

*Lysistrata.* I laugh at them. Neither threats nor flames shall force our doors; they shall open only on the conditions I have named.

*Calonicé.* Yes, yes, by Aphrodité! let us keep up our old-time repute for obstinacy and spite.

*Chorus of Old Men.* Go easy, Draces, go easy; why, your shoulder is all chafed by these plaguey heavy olive stocks. But forward still, forward, man, as needs must. What unlooked-for things do happen, to be sure, in a long life! Ah! Strymodorus, who would ever have thought it? Here we have the women, who used, for our misfortune, to eat our bread and live in our houses, daring nowadays to lay hands on the holy image of the goddess, to seize the Acropolis and draw bars and bolts to keep any from entering! Come, Philurgus man, let's hurry thither; let's lay our faggots all about the citadel, and on the blazing pile burn with our hands these vile conspiratresses, one and all—and Lycon's wife, Lysistrata, first and foremost! Nay, by Demeter, never will I let 'em laugh at me, whiles I have a breath left in my body. Cleomenes himself, the first who ever seized our citadel, had to quit it to his sore dishonour; spite his Lacedaemo-

nian pride, he had to deliver me up his arms and slink
off with a single garment to his back. My word! but he
was filthy and ragged! and what an unkempt beard, to
be sure! He had not had a bath for six long years! Oh!
but that was a mighty siege! Our men were ranged sev-
enteen deep before the gate, and never left their posts,
even to sleep. These women, these enemies of Euripides
and all the gods, shall I do nothing to hinder their in-
ordinate insolence? else let them tear down my trophies
of Marathon. But look ye, to finish our toilsome climb,
we have only this last steep bit left to mount. Verily 'tis
no easy job without beasts of burden, and how these
logs do bruise my shoulder! Still let us on, and blow up
our fire and see it does not go out just as we reach our
destination. Phew! phew! (*blows the fire.*) Oh! dear!
what a dreadful smoke! it bites my eyes like a mad dog.
It is Lemnos fire for sure, or it would never devour my
eyelids like this. Come on, Laches, let's hurry, let's bring
succour to the goddess; it's now or never! Phew! phew!
(*blows the fire.*) Oh! dear! what a confounded smoke!
—There now, there's our fire all bright and burning,
thank the gods! Now, why not first put down our loads
here, then take a vine-branch, light it at the brazier and
hurl it at the gate by way of battering-ram? If they don't
answer our summons by pulling back the bolts, then we
set fire to the woodwork, and the smoke will choke 'em.
Ye gods! what a smoke! Pfaugh! Is there never a Samos
general will help me unload my burden?—Ah! it shall
not gall my shoulder any more. (*Tosses down his wood.*)
Come, brazier, do your duty, make the embers flare, that
I may kindle a brand; I want to be the first to hurl one.
Aid me, heavenly Victory; let us punish for their insolent
audacity the women who have seized our citadel, and
may we raise a trophy of triumph for success!

*Chorus of Women.* Oh! my dears, methinks I see fire
and smoke; can it be a conflagration? Let us hurry all we

can. Fly, fly, Nicodicé, ere Calycé and Crityllé perish in the fire, or are stifled in the smoke raised by these accursed old men and their pitiless laws. But, great gods, can it be I come too late? Rising at dawn, I had the utmost trouble to fill this vessel at the fountain. Oh! what a crowd there was, and what a din! What a rattling of water-pots! Servants and slave-girls pushed and thronged me! However, here I have it full at last; and I am running to carry the water to my fellow-townswomen, whom our foes are plotting to burn alive. News has been brought us that a company of old, doddering greybeards, loaded with enormous faggots, as if they wanted to heat a furnace, have taken the field, vomiting dreadful threats, crying that they must reduce to ashes these horrible women. Suffer them not, oh! goddess, but, of thy grace, may I see Athens and Greece cured of their warlike folly. 'Tis to this end, oh! thou guardian deity of our city, goddess of the golden crest, that they have seized thy sanctuary. Be their friend and ally, Athené, and if any man hurl against them lighted fire-brands, aid us to carry water to extinguish them.

*Stratyllis.* Let me be, I say. Oh! oh! (*She calls for help.*)

*Chorus of Women.* What is this I see, ye wretched old men? Honest and pious folk ye cannot be who act so vilely.

*Chorus of Old Men.* Ah, ha! here's something new! a swarm of women stand posted outside to defend the gates!

*Chorus of Women.* Ah! ah! we frighten you, do we; we seem a mighty host, yet you do not see the ten-thousandth part of our sex.

*Chorus of Old Men.* Ho, Phaedrias! shall we stop their cackle? Suppose one of us were to break a stick across their backs, eh?

*Chorus of Women.* Let us set down our water-pots on

24

the ground, to be out of the way, if they should dare to offer us violence.

*Chorus of Old Men.* Let someone knock out two or three teeth for them, as they did to Bupalus; they won't talk so loud then.

*Chorus of Women.* Come on then; I wait you with unflinching foot, and I will snap you off like a bitch.

*Chorus of Old Men.* Silence! ere my stick has cut short your days.

*Chorus of Women.* Now, just you dare to touch Stratyllis with the tip of your finger!

*Chorus of Old Men.* And if I batter you to pieces with my fists, what will you do?

*Chorus of Women.* I will tear out your lungs and entrails with my teeth.

*Chorus of Old Men.* Oh! what a clever poet is Euripides! how well he says that woman is the most shameless of animals.

*Chorus of Women.* Let's pick up our water-jars again, Rhodippé.

*Chorus of Old Men.* Ah! accursed harlot, what do you mean to do here with your water?

*Chorus of Women.* And you, old death-in-life, with your fire? Is it to cremate yourself?

*Chorus of Old Men.* I am going to build you a pyre to roast your female friends upon.

*Chorus of Women.* And I,—I am going to put out your fire.

*Chorus of Old Men.* You put out my fire—you!

*Chorus of Women.* Yes, you shall soon see.

*Chorus of Old Men.* I don't know what prevents me from roasting you with this torch.

*Chorus of Women.* I am getting you a bath ready to clean off the filth.

*Chorus of Old Men.* A bath for me, you dirty slut, you!

*Chorus of Women.* Yes, indeed, a nuptial bath—he, he!

*Chorus of Old Men.* Do you hear that? What insolence!

*Chorus of Women.* I am a free woman, I tell you.

*Chorus of Old Men.* I will make you hold your tongue, never fear!

*Chorus of Women.* Ah, ha! you shall never sit more amongst the Heliasts.

*Chorus of Old Men.* Burn off her hair for her!

*Chorus of Women.* Water, do your office! (*The women pitch the water in their water-pots over the old men.*)

*Chorus of Old Men.* Oh, dear! oh, dear! oh, dear!

*Chorus of Women.* Was it hot?

*Chorus of Old Men.* Hot, great gods! Enough, enough!

*Chorus of Women.* I'm watering you, to make you bloom afresh.

*Chorus of Old Men.* Alas! I am too dry! Ah, me! how I am trembling with cold!

*Magistrate.* These women, have they made din enough, I wonder, with their tambourines? bewept Adonis enough upon their terraces? I was listening to the speeches last assembly day, and Demostratus, whom heaven confound! was saying we must all go over to Sicily—and lo! his wife was dancing round repeating: Alas! alas! Adonis, woe is me for Adonis!

Demostratus was saying we must levy hoplites at Zacynthus—and lo! his wife, more than half drunk, was screaming on the house-roof: "Weep, weep for Adonis!" —while that infamous *Mad Ox* was bellowing away on his side.—Do ye not blush, ye women, for your wild and uproarious doings?

*Chorus of Old Men.* But you don't know all their effrontery yet! They abused and insulted us; then soused us with the water in their water-pots, and have set us wringing out our clothes, for all the world as if we had bepissed ourselves.

*Magistrate.* And 'tis well done too, by Posidon! We men must share the blame of their ill conduct; it is we who teach them to love riot and dissoluteness and sow the seeds of wickedness in their hearts. You see a husband go into a shop: "Look you, jeweler," says he, "you remember the necklace you made for my wife. Well, t'other evening, when she was dancing, the catch came open. Now, I am bound to start for Salamis; will you make it convenient to go up to-night to make her fastening secure?" Another will go to a cobbler, a great, strong fellow, with a great, long tool, and tell him: "The strap of one of my wife's sandals presses her little toe, which is extremely sensitive; come in about midday to supple the thing and stretch it." Now see the results. Take my own case—as a Magistrate I have enlisted rowers; I want money to pay 'em, and lo! the women clap to the door in my face. But why do we stand here with arms crossed? Bring me a crowbar; I'll chastise their insolence!—Ho! there, my fine fellow! (*addressing one of his attendant officers*) what are you gaping at the crows about? looking for a tavern, I suppose, eh? Come, crowbars here, and force open the gates. I will put a hand to the work myself.

*Lysistrata.* No need to force the gates; I am coming out —here I am. And why bolts and bars? What we want here is not bolts and bars and locks, but common sense.

*Magistrate.* Really, my fine lady! Where is my officer? I want him to tie that woman's hands behind her back.

*Lysistrata.* By Artemis, the virgin goddess! if he touches me with the tip of his finger, officer of the public peace though he be, let him look out for himself!

*Magistrate* (*to the officer*). How now, are you afraid? Seize her, I tell you, round the body. Two of you at her, and have done with it!

*First Woman.* By Pandrosos! if you lay a hand on her, I'll trample you underfoot till you spill your guts!

*Magistrate.* Oh, there! my guts! Where is my other officer? Bind that minx first, who speaks so prettily!

*Second Woman.* By Phoebé, if you touch her with one finger, you'd better call quick for a surgeon!

*Magistrate.* What do you mean? Officer, where are you got to? Lay hold of her. Oh! but I'm going to stop your foolishness for you all!

*Third Woman.* By the Tauric Artemis, if you go near her, I'll pull out your hair, scream as you like.

*Magistrate.* Ah! miserable man that I am! My own officers desert me. What ho! are we to let ourselves be bested by a mob of women? Ho! Scythians mine, close up your ranks, and forward!

*Lysistrata.* By the holy goddesses! you'll have to make acquaintance with four companies of women, ready for the fray and well armed to boot.

*Magistrate.* Forward, Scythians, and bind them!

*Lysistrata.* Forward, my gallant companions; march forth, ye vendors of grain and eggs, garlic and vegetables, keepers of taverns and bakeries, wrench and strike and tear; come, a torrent of invective and insult! (*They beat the officers.*) Enough, enough! now retire, never rob the vanquished!

*Magistrate.* Here's a fine exploit for my officers!

*Lysistrata.* Ah, ha! so you thought you had only to do with a set of slave-women! you did not know the ardour that fills the bosom of free-born dames.

*Magistrate.* Ardour! yes, by Apollo, ardour enough— especially for the wine-cup!

*Chorus of Old Men.* Sir, sir! what use of words? they are of no avail with wild beasts of this sort. Don't you know how they have just washed us down—and with no very fragrant soap!

*Chorus of Women.* What would you have? You should never have laid rash hands on us. If you start afresh, I'll knock your eyes out. My delight is to stay at home as coy as a young maid, without hurting anybody or moving any more than a milestone; but 'ware the wasps, if you go stirring up the wasps' nest!

*Chorus of Old Men.* Ah! great gods! how get the better of these ferocious creatures? 'tis past all bearing! But come, let us try to find out the reason of the dreadful scourge. With what end in view have they seized the citadel of Cranaus, the sacred shrine that is raised upon the inaccessible rock of the Acropolis? Question them; be cautious and not too credulous. 'Twould be culpable negligence not to pierce the mystery, if we may.

*Magistrate (addressing the women).* I would ask you first why ye have barred our gates.

*Lysistrata.* To seize the treasury; no more money, no more war.

*Magistrate.* Then money is the cause of the War?

*Lysistrata.* And of all our troubles. 'Twas to find occasion to steal that Pisander and all the other agitators were forever raising revolutions. Well and good! but they'll never get another drachma here.

*Magistrate.* What do you propose to do then, pray?

*Lysistrata.* You ask me that! Why, we propose to administer the treasury ourselves.

*Magistrate. You* do?

*Lysistrata.* What is there in that to surprise you? Do we not administer the budget of household expenses?

*Magistrate.* But that is not the same thing.

*Lysistrata.* How so—not the same thing?

*Magistrate.* It is the treasury supplies the expenses of the War.

*Lysistrata.* That's our first principle—no War!

*Magistrate.* What! and the safety of the city?

*Lysistrata.* We will provide for that.

*Magistrate. You?*

*Lysistrata.* Yes, just we.

*Magistrate.* What a sorry business!

*Lysistrata.* Yes, we're going to save you, whether you will or no.

*Magistrate.* Oh! the impudence of the creatures!

*Lysistrata.* You seem annoyed! but there, you've got to come to it.

*Magistrate.* But 'tis the very height of iniquity!

*Lysistrata.* We're going to save you, my man.

*Magistrate.* But if I don't want to be saved?

*Lysistrata.* Why, all the more reason!

*Magistrate.* But what a notion, to concern yourselves with questions of Peace and War!

*Lysistrata.* We will explain our idea.

*Magistrate.* Out with it then; quick, or . . . (*threatening her*).

*Lysistrata.* Listen, and never a movement, please!

*Magistrate.* Oh! it is too much for me! I cannot keep my temper!

*A Woman.* Then look out for yourself; you have more to fear than we have.

*Magistrate.* Stop your croaking, old crow, you! (*To Lysistrata.*) Now you, say your say.

*Lysistrata.* Willingly. All the long time the War has lasted, we have endured in modest silence all you men did; we never allowed ourselves to open our lips. We were far from satisfied, for we knew how things were going; often in our homes we would hear you discussing, upside down and inside out, some important turn of affairs. Then with sad hearts, but smiling lips, we would ask you: Well, in to-day's Assembly did they vote Peace? —But, "Mind your own business!" the husband would growl, "Hold your tongue, do!" And I would say no more.

*A Woman.* I would not have held my tongue though, not I!

*Magistrate.* You would have been reduced to silence by blows then.

*Lysistrata.* Well, for my part, I would say no more. But

presently I would come to know you had arrived at some fresh decision more fatally foolish than ever. "Ah! my dear man," I would say, "what madness next!" But he would only look at me askance and say: "Just weave your web, do; else your cheeks will smart for hours. War is men's business!"

*Magistrate.* Bravo! well said indeed!

*Lysistrata.* How now, wretched man? not to let us contend against your follies, was bad enough! But presently we heard you asking out loud in the open street: "Is there never a man left in Athens?" and, "No, not one, not one," you were assured in reply. Then, then we made up our minds without more delay to make common cause to save Greece. Open your ears to our wise counsels and hold your tongues, and we may yet put things on a better footing.

*Magistrate. You* put things indeed! Oh! 'tis too much! The insolence of the creatures! Silence, I say.

*Lysistrata.* Silence yourself!

*Magistrate.* May I die a thousand deaths ere I obey one who wears a veil!

*Lysistrata.* If that's all that troubles you, here, take my veil, wrap it round your head, and hold your tongue. Then take this basket; put on a girdle, card wool, munch beans. The War shall be women's business.

*Chorus of Women.* Lay aside your water-pots, we will guard them, we will help our friends and companions. For myself, I will never weary of the dance; my knees will never grow stiff with fatigue. I will brave everything with my dear allies, on whom Nature has lavished virtue, grace, boldness, cleverness, and whose wisely directed energy is going to save the State. Oh! my good, gallant Lysistrata, and all my friends, be ever like a bundle of nettles; never let your anger slacken; the winds of fortune blow our way.

*Lysistrata.* May gentle Love and the sweet Cyprian

Queen shower seductive charms on our bosoms and all our person. If only we may stir so amorous a feeling among the men that they stand firm as sticks, we shall indeed deserve the name of peace-makers among the Greeks.

*Magistrate.* How will that be, pray?

*Lysistrata.* To begin with, we shall not see you any more running like mad fellows to the Market holding lance in fist.

*A Woman.* That will be something gained, anyway, by the Paphian goddess, it will!

*Lysistrata.* Now we see 'em, mixed up with saucepans and kitchen stuff, armed to the teeth, looking like wild Corybantes!

*Magistrate.* Why, of course; that's how brave men should do.

*Lysistrata.* Oh! but what a funny sight, to behold a man wearing a Gorgon's-head buckler coming along to buy fish!

*A Woman.* T'other day in the Market I saw a phylarch with flowing ringlets; he was a-horseback, and was pouring into his helmet the broth he had just bought at an old dame's still. There was a Thracian warrior too, who was brandishing his lance like Tereus in the play; he had scared a good woman selling figs into a perfect panic, and was gobbling up all her ripest fruit.

*Magistrate.* And how, pray, would you propose to restore peace and order in all the countries of Greece?

*Lysistrata.* 'Tis the easiest thing in the world!

*Magistrate.* Come, tell us how; I am curious to know.

*Lysistrata.* When we are winding thread, and it is tangled, we pass the spool across and through the skein, now this way, now that way; even so, to finish off the War, we shall send embassies hither and thither and everywhere, to disentangle matters.

*Magistrate.* And 'tis with your yarn, and your skeins,

and your spools, you think to appease so many bitter enmities, you silly women?

*Lysistrata.* If only you had common sense, you would always do in politics the same as we do with our yarn.

*Magistrate.* Come, how is that, eh?

*Lysistrata.* First we wash the yarn to separate the grease and filth; do the same with all bad citizens, sort them out and drive them forth with rods—'tis the refuse of the city. Then for all such as come crowding up in search of employments and offices, we must card them thoroughly; then, to bring them all to the same standard, pitch them pell-mell into the same basket, resident aliens or no, allies, debtors to the State, all mixed up together. Then as for our Colonies, you must think of them as so many isolated hanks; find the ends of the separate threads, draw them to a centre here, wind them into one, make one great hank of the lot, out of which the Public can weave itself a good, stout tunic.

*Magistrate.* Is it not a sin and a shame to see them carding and winding the State, these women who have neither art nor part in the burdens of the War?

*Lysistrata.* What! wretched man! why, 'tis a far heavier burden to us than to you. In the first place, we bear sons who go off to fight far away from Athens.

*Magistrate.* Enough said! do not recall sad and sorry memories!

*Lysistrata.* Then secondly, instead of enjoying the pleasures of love and making the best of our youth and beauty, we are left to languish far from our husbands, who are all with the army. But say no more of ourselves; what afflicts me is to see our girls growing old in lonely grief.

*Magistrate.* Don't the men grow old too?

*Lysistrata.* That is not the same thing. When the soldier returns from the wars, even though he has white hair, he very soon finds a young wife. But a woman has only one summer; if she does not make hay while the sun shines, no one will afterwards have anything to say to her, and she spends her days consulting oracles that never send her a husband.

*Magistrate.* But the old man who can still do it . . .

*Lysistrata.* But you, why don't you get done with it and die? You are rich; go buy yourself a bier, and I will knead you a honey-cake for Cerberus. Here, take this garland. (*Drenching him with water.*)

*First Woman.* And this one too. (*Drenching him with water.*)

*Second Woman.* And these fillets. (*Drenching him with water.*)

*Lysistrata.* What do you lack more? Step aboard the boat; Charon is waiting for you, you're keeping him from pushing off.

*Magistrate.* To treat me so scurvily! What an insult! I will go show myself to my fellow-magistrates just as I am.

*Lysistrata.* What! are you blaming us for not having exposed you according to custom? Nay, console yourself; we will not fail to offer up the third-day sacrifice for you, first thing in the morning.

*Chorus of Old Men.* Awake, friends of freedom; let us hold ourselves aye ready to act. I suspect a mighty peril; I foresee another Tyranny like Hippias'. I am sore afraid the Laconians assembled here with Cleisthenes have, by a stratagem of war, stirred up these women, enemies of the gods, to seize upon our treasury and the funds whereby I lived. Is it not a sin and a shame for them to interfere in advising the citizens, to prate of shields and lances, and to ally themselves with Laconians, fellows I trust no more than I would so many famished wolves? The whole thing, my friends, is nothing else but an attempt to re-establish Tyranny. But I will never submit; I will be on my guard for the future; I will always carry a blade hidden under myrtle boughs; I will post myself in the Public Square under arms, shoulder to shoulder with Aristogiton; and now, to make a start, I must just break a few of that cursed old jade's teeth yonder.

*Chorus of Women.* Nay, never play the brave man, else when you go back home, your own mother won't know you. But, dear friends and allies, first let us lay our burdens down; then, citizens all, hear what I have to say. I have useful counsel to give our city, which deserves it well at my hands for the brilliant distinctions it has lavished on my girlhood. At seven years of age, I was bearer of the sacred vessels; at ten, I pounded barley for the altar of Athené; next, clad in a robe of yellow silk, I was *little bear* to Artemis at the Brauronia; presently, grown a tall, handsome maiden, they put a necklace of dried figs about my neck, and I was Basket-Bearer. So surely I am bound to give my best advice to Athens. What matters that I was born a woman, if I can cure your misfortunes? I pay my share of tolls and taxes, by giving men to the State. But you, you miserable greybeards, you contribute nothing to the public charges; on the contrary, you have wasted the treasure of our forefathers, as it was called, the treasure amassed in the days of the Persian Wars. You pay nothing at all in return; and into the bargain you endanger our lives and liberties by your mistakes. Have you one word to say for yourselves? . . . Ah! don't irritate me, you there, or I'll lay my slipper across your jaws; and it's pretty heavy.

*Chorus of Old Men.* Outrage upon outrage! things are going from bad to worse. Let us punish the minxes, every one of us that has a man's appendages to boast of. Come, off with our tunics, for a man must savour of manhood; come, my friends, let us strip naked from head to foot. Courage, I say, we who in our day garrisoned Lipsydrion; let us be young again, and shake off eld. If we give them the least hold over us, 'tis all up; their audacity will know no bounds! We shall see them building ships, and fighting sea-fights, like Artemisia; nay, if they want to mount and ride as cavalry, we had best cashier the knights, for indeed women excel in riding, and have a fine, firm seat for the gallop. Just think of all those squadrons of Amazons Micon has painted for us engaged in hand-to-hand combat with men. Come then, we must e'en fit collars to all these willing necks.

*Chorus of Women.* By the blessed goddesses, if you anger me, I will let loose the beast of my evil passions, and a very hailstorm of blows will set you yelling for help. Come, dames, off tunics, and quick's the word; women must scent the savour of women in the throes of passion. . . . Now just you dare to measure strength with me, old greybeard, and I warrant you you'll never eat garlic or black beans more. No, not a word! my anger is at boiling point, and I'll do with you what the beetle did with the eagle's eggs.

I laugh at your threats, so long as I have on my side Lampito here, and the noble Theban, my dear Ismenia. . . . Pass decree on decree, you can do us no hurt, you wretch abhorred of all your fellows. Why, only yesterday, on occasion of the feast of Hecaté, I asked my neighbours of Boeotia for one of their daughters for whom my girls have a lively liking—a fine, fat eel to wit; and if they did not refuse, all along of your silly decrees! We shall never cease to suffer the like, till someone gives you a neat trip-up and breaks your neck for you!

(*Several days are supposed to have elapsed*)

*Chorus of Women* (*addressing Lysistrata*). You, Lysistrata, you who are leader of our glorious enterprise, why do I see you coming towards me with so gloomy an air?

*Lysistrata.* 'Tis the behaviour of these naughty women, 'tis the female heart and female weakness so discourages me.

*Chorus of Women.* Tell us, tell us, what is it?

*Lysistrata.* I only tell the simple truth.

*Chorus of Women.* What has happened so disconcerting? Come, tell your friends.

*Lysistrata.* Oh! the thing is so hard to tell—yet so impossible to conceal.

*Chorus of Women.* Nay, never seek to hide any ill that has befallen our cause.

*Lysistrata.* To blurt it out in a word—we are in passion!

*Chorus of Women.* Oh! Zeus, oh! Zeus!

*Lysistrata.* What use calling upon Zeus? The thing is even as I say. I cannot stop them any longer from lusting after the men. They are all for deserting. The first I caught was slipping out by the postern gate near the cave of Pan; another was letting herself down by a rope and pulley; a third was busy preparing her escape; while a fourth, perched on a bird's back, was just taking wing for Orsilochus' house, when I seized her by the hair. One and all, they are inventing excuses to be off home. Look! there goes one, trying to get out! Halloa there! whither away so fast?

*First Woman.* I want to go home; I have some Miletus wool in the house, which is getting all eaten up by worms.

*Lysistrata.* Bah! you and your worms! go back, I say!

*First Woman.* I will return immediately, I swear I will by the two goddesses! I only have just to spread it out on the bed.

*Lysistrata.* You shall not do anything of the kind! I say, you shall not go.

*First Woman.* Must I leave my wool to spoil then?

*Lysistrata.* Yes, if need be.

*Second Woman.* Unhappy woman that I am! Alas for my flax! I've left it at home unstript!

*Lysistrata.* So, here's another trying to escape to go home and strip her flax forsooth!

*Second Woman.* Oh! I swear by the goddess of light,

the instant I have put it in condition I will come straight back.

*Lysistrata.* You shall do nothing of the kind! If once you began, others would want to follow suit.

*Third Woman.* Oh! goddess divine, Ilithyia, patroness of women in labour, stay, stay the birth, till I have reached a spot less hallowed than Athené's Mount!

*Lysistrata.* What mean you by these silly tales?

*Third Woman.* I am going to have a child—now, this minute.

*Lysistrata.* But you were not pregnant yesterday!

*Third Woman.* Well, I am to-day. Oh! let me go in search of the midwife, Lysistrata, quick, quick!

*Lysistrata.* What is this fable you are telling me? Ah! what have you got there so hard?

*Third Woman.* A male child.

*Lysistrata.* No, no, by Aphrodité! nothing of the sort! Why, it feels like something hollow—a pot or a kettle. Oh! you baggage, if you have not got the sacred helmet of Pallas—and you said you were with child!

*Third Woman.* And so I am, by Zeus, I am!

*Lysistrata.* Then why this helmet, pray?

*Third Woman.* For fear my pains should seize me in the Acropolis; I mean to lay my eggs in this helmet, as the doves do.

*Lysistrata.* Excuses and pretences every word! the thing's as clear as daylight. Anyway, you must stay here now till the fifth day, your day of purification.

*Third Woman.* I cannot sleep any more in the Acropolis, now I have seen the snake that guards the Temple.

*Fourth Woman.* Ah! and those confounded owls with their dismal hooting! I cannot get a wink of rest, and I'm just dying of fatigue.

*Lysistrata.* You wicked women, have done with your falsehoods! You want your husbands, that's plain enough. But don't you think they want you just as badly? They are spending dreadful nights, oh! I know that well enough. But hold out, my dears, hold out! A little more patience, and the victory will be ours. An Oracle promises us success, if only we remain united. Shall I repeat the words?

*First Woman.* Yes, tell us what the Oracle declares.

*Lysistrata.* Silence then! Now—"Whenas the swallows, fleeing before the hoopoes, shall have all flocked together in one place, and shall refrain from all amorous commerce, then will be the end of all the ills of life; yea, and Zeus, which doth thunder in the skies, shall set above what was erst below. . . ."

*Chorus of Women.* What! shall the men be underneath?

*Lysistrata.* "But if dissension do arise among the swallows, and they take wing from the holy Temple, 'twill be said there is never a more wanton bird in all the world."

*Chorus of Women.* Ye gods! the prophecy is clear. Nay, never let us be cast down by calamity! let us be brave to bear, and go back to our posts. 'Twere shameful indeed not to trust the promises of the Oracle.

*Chorus of Old Men.* I want to tell you a fable they used to relate to me when I was a little boy. This is it: Once upon a time there was a young man called Melanion, who hated the thought of marriage so sorely that he fled away to the wilds. So he dwelt in the mountains, wove himself nets, kept a dog and caught hares. He never, never came back, he had such a horror of women. As chaste as Melanion, we loathe the jades just as much as he did.

*An Old Man.* You dear old woman, I would fain kiss you.

*A Woman.* I will set you crying without onions.

*Old Man.* . . . And give you a sound kicking.

*A Woman.* Ah, ha! what a dense forest you have there! (*Pointing.*)

*Old Man.* So was Myronides one of the best-bearded

39

of men o' this side; his backside was all black, and he terrified his enemies as much as Phormio.

*Chorus of Women.* I want to tell you a fable too, to match yours about Melanion. Once there was a certain man called Timon, a tough customer, and a whimsical, a true son of the Furies, with a face that seemed to glare out of a thorn-bush. He withdrew from the world because he couldn't abide bad men, after vomiting a thousand curses at 'em. He had a holy horror of ill-conditioned fellows, but he was mighty tender towards women.

*A Woman.* Suppose I up and broke your jaw for you!

*Old Man.* I am not a bit afraid of you.

*A Woman.* Suppose I let fly a good kick at you?

*Old Man.* I should see your backside then.

*Woman.* You would see that, for all my age, it is very well attended to.

*Lysistrata.* Ho there! come quick, come quick!

*First Woman.* What is it? Why these cries?

*Lysistrata.* A man! a man! I see him approaching all afire with the flames of love. Oh! divine Queen of Cyprus, Paphos and Cythera, I pray you still be propitious to our emprise.

*First Woman.* Where is he, this unknown foe?

*Lysistrata.* Yonder—beside the Temple of Demeter.

*First Woman.* Yes, indeed, I see him; but who is it?

*Lysistrata.* Look, look! does any of you recognize him?

*First Woman.* I do, I do! 'tis my husband Cinesias.

*Lysistrata.* To work then! Be it your task to inflame and torture and torment him. Seductions, caresses, provocations, refusals, try every means! Grant every favour, —always excepting what is forbidden by our oath on the wine-bowl.

*Myrrhiné.* Have no fear, I undertake the work.

*Lysistrata.* Well, I will stay here to help you cajole the man and set his passions aflame. The rest of you, withdraw.

*Cinesias.* Alas! alas! how I am tortured by spasm and rigid convulsion! Oh! I am racked on the wheel!

*Lysistrata.* Who is this that dares to pass our lines?

*Cinesias.* It is I.

*Lysistrata.* What, a man?

*Cinesias.* Yes, no doubt about it, a man!

*Lysistrata.* Begone!

*Cinesias.* But who are you that thus repulses me?

*Lysistrata.* The sentinel of the day.

*Cinesias.* By all the gods, call Myrrhiné hither.

*Lysistrata.* Call Myrrhiné hither, quotha? And pray, who are you?

*Cinesias.* I am her husband, Cinesias, son of Peon.

*Lysistrata.* Ah! good day, my dear friend. Your name is not unknown amongst us. Your wife has it forever on her lips; and she never touches an egg or an apple without saying: "'Twill be for Cinesias."

*Cinesias.* Really and truly?

*Lysistrata.* Yes, indeed, by Aphrodité! And if we fall to talking of men, quick your wife declares: "Oh! all the rest, they're good for nothing compared with Cinesias."

*Cinesias.* Oh! I beseech you, go and call her to me.

*Lysistrata.* And what will you give me for my trouble?

*Cinesias.* Anything I've got, if you like. I will give you what I have there!

*Lysistrata.* Well, well, I will tell her to come.

*Cinesias.* Quick, oh! be quick! Life has no more charms for me since she left my house. I am sad, sad, when I go indoors; it all seems so empty; my victuals have lost their savour. Desire is eating out my heart!

*Myrrhiné.* I love him, oh! I love him; but he won't let himself be loved. No! I shall not come.

*Cinesias.* Myrrhiné, my little darling Myrrhiné, what are you saying? Come down to me quick.

*Myrrhiné.* No indeed, not I.

41

*Cinesias.* I call you, Myrrhiné, Myrrhiné; will you not come?

*Myrrhiné.* Why should you call me? You do not want me.

*Cinesias.* Not want you! Why, here I stand, stiff with desire!

*Myrrhiné.* Good-bye.

*Cinesias.* Oh! Myrrhiné, Myrrhiné, in our child's name, hear me; at any rate hear the child! Little lad, call your mother.

*Child.* Mammy, mammy, mammy!

*Cinesias.* There, listen! Don't you pity the poor child? It's six days now you've never washed and never fed the child.

*Myrrhiné.* Poor darling, your father takes mighty little care of you!

*Cinesias.* Come down, dearest, come down for the child's sake.

*Myrrhiné.* Ah! what a thing it is to be a mother! Well, well, we must come down, I suppose.

*Cinesias.* Why, how much younger and prettier she looks! And how she looks at me so lovingly! Her cruelty and scorn only redouble my passion.

*Myrrhiné.* You are as sweet as your father is provoking! Let me kiss you, my treasure, mother's darling!

*Cinesias.* Ah! what a bad thing it is to let yourself be led away by other women! Why give me such pain and suffering, and yourself into the bargain?

*Myrrhiné.* Hands off, sir!

*Cinesias.* Everything is going to rack and ruin in the house.

*Myrrhiné.* I don't care.

*Cinesias.* But your web that's all being pecked to pieces by the cocks and hens, don't you care for that?

*Myrrhiné.* Precious little.

*Cinesias.* And Aphrodité, whose mysteries you have

not celebrated for so long? Oh! won't you come back home?

*Myrrhiné.* No, at least, not till a sound Treaty put an end to the War.

*Cinesias.* Well, if you wish it so much, why, we'll make it, your Treaty.

*Myrrhiné.* Well and good! When that's done, I will come home. Till then, I am bound by an oath.

*Cinesias.* At any rate, let's have a short time together.

*Myrrhiné.* No, no, no! . . . all the same I cannot say I don't love you.

*Cinesias.* You love me? Then why refuse what I ask, my little girl, my sweet Myrrhiné?

*Myrrhiné.* You must be joking! What, before the child!

*Cinesias.* Manes, carry the lad home. There, you see, the child is gone; there's nothing to hinder us; let us to work!

*Myrrhiné.* But, miserable man, where, where?

*Cinesias.* In the cave of Pan; nothing could be better.

*Myrrhiné.* But how to purify myself, before going back into the citadel?

*Cinesias.* Nothing easier! you can wash at the Clepsydra.

*Myrrhiné.* But my oath? Do you want me to perjure myself?

*Cinesias.* I take all responsibility; never make yourself anxious.

*Myrrhiné.* Well, I'll be off, then, and find a bed for us.

*Cinesias.* Oh! 'tis not worth while; we can lie on the ground surely.

*Myrrhiné.* No, no! bad man as you are, I don't like your lying on the bare earth.

*Cinesias.* Ah! how the dear girl loves me!

*Myrrhiné* (*coming back with a bed*). Come, get to bed quick; I am going to undress. But, plague take it, we must get a mattress.

*Cinesias.* A mattress! Oh! no, never mind!

*Myrrhiné.* No, by Artemis! lie on the bare sacking, never! That were too squalid.

*Cinesias.* A kiss!

*Myrrhiné.* Wait a minute!

*Cinesias.* Oh! by the great gods, be quick back!

*Myrrhiné.* Here is a mattress. Lie down, I am just going to undress. But, but you've got no pillow.

*Cinesias.* I don't want one, no, no.

*Myrrhiné.* But *I* do.

*Cinesias.* Oh, dear, oh, dear! they treat my poor self for all the world like Heracles.

*Myrrhiné (coming back with a pillow).* There, lift your head, dear!

*Cinesias.* That's really everything.

*Myrrhiné.* Is it everything, I wonder.

*Cinesias.* Come, my treasure.

*Myrrhiné.* I am just unfastening my girdle. But remember what you promised me about making peace; mind you keep your word.

*Cinesias.* Yes, yes, upon my life I will.

*Myrrhiné.* Why, you have no blanket.

*Cinesias.* Great Zeus! what matter of that? 'tis you I want to love.

*Myrrhiné.* Never fear—directly, directly! I'll be back in no time.

*Cinesias.* The woman will kill me with her blankets!

*Myrrhiné (coming back with a blanket).* Now get up for one moment.

*Cinesias.* But I tell you, our friend here is all ready!

*Myrrhiné.* Would you like me to scent you?

*Cinesias.* No, by Apollo, no, please!

*Myrrhiné.* Yes, by Aphrodité, but I will, whether you wish it or no.

*Cinesias.* Ah! great Zeus, may she soon be done!

*Myrrhiné (coming back with a flask of perfume).* Hold out your hand; now rub it in.

*Cinesias.* Oh! in Apollo's name, I don't much like the smell of it; but perhaps 'twill improve when it's well rubbed in. It does not somehow smack of the marriage bed!

*Myrrhiné.* There, what a scatterbrain I am; if I have not brought Rhodian perfumes!

*Cinesias.* Never mind, dearest, let be now.

*Myrrhiné.* You are joking!

*Cinesias.* Deuce take the man who first invented perfumes, say I!

*Myrrhiné (coming back with another flask).* Here, take this bottle.

*Cinesias.* I have a better all ready for your service, darling. Come, you provoking creature, to bed with you, and don't bring another thing.

*Myrrhiné.* Coming, coming; I'm just slipping off my shoes. Dear boy, will you vote for peace?

*Cinesias.* I'll think about it. *(Myrrhiné runs away.)* I'm a dead man, she is killing me! She has gone, and left me in torment! I must have someone to love, I must! Ah me! the loveliest of women has choused and cheated me. Poor little lad, how am I to give you what you want so badly? Where is Cynalopex? quick, man, get him a nurse, do!

*Chorus of Old Men.* Poor, miserable wretch, baulked in your amorousness! what tortures are yours! Ah! you fill me with pity. Could any man's back and loins stand such a strain. He stands stiff and rigid, and there's never a wench to help him!

*Cinesias.* Ye gods in heaven, what pains I suffer!

*Chorus of Old Men.* Well, there it is; 'tis her doing, that abandoned hussy!

*Cinesias.* Nay, nay! rather say that sweetest, dearest darling.

*Chorus of Old Men.* That dearest darling? no, no, that hussy, say I! Zeus, thou god of the skies, canst not let loose a hurricane, to sweep them all up into the air, and whirl 'em round, then drop 'em down crash! and impale them on the point of his weapon!

*A Herald.* Say, where shall I find the Senate and the Prytanes? I am bearer of despatches.

*Magistrate.* But are you a man or a Priapus, pray?

*Herald.* Oh! but he's mighty simple. I am a herald, of course, I swear I am, and I come from Sparta about making peace.

*Magistrate.* But look, you are hiding a lance under your clothes, surely.

*Herald.* No, nothing of the sort.

*Magistrate.* Then why do you turn away like that, and hold your cloak out from your body? Have you gotten swellings in the groin with your journey?

*Herald.* By the twin brethren! the man's an old maniac.

*Magistrate.* Ah, ha! my fine lad, why I can see it standing, oh fie!

*Herald.* I tell you no! but enough of this foolery.

*Magistrate.* Well, what is it you have there then?

*Herald.* A Lacedaemonian 'skytalé.'

*Magistrate.* Oh, indeed, a 'skytalé,' is it? Well, well, speak out frankly; I know all about these matters. How are things going at Sparta now?

*Herald.* Why, everything is turned upside down at Sparta; and all the allies are half dead with lusting. We simply must have Pellené.

*Magistrate.* What is the reason of it all? Is it the god Pan's doing?

*Herald.* No, but Lampito's and the Spartan women's, acting at her instigation; they have denied the men all access to them.

*Magistrate.* But whatever do you do?

46

*Herald.* We are at our wits' end; we walk bent double, just as if we were carrying lanterns in a wind. The jades have sworn we shall not so much as touch them till we have all agreed to conclude peace.

*Magistrate.* Ha, ha! So I see now, 'tis a general conspiracy embracing all Greece. Go you back to Sparta and bid them send Envoys with plenary powers to treat for peace. I will urge our Senators myself to name Plenipotentiaries from us; and to persuade them, why, I will show them something else.

*Herald.* What could be better? I fly at your command.

*Chorus of Old Men.* No wild beast is there, no flame of fire, more fierce and untamable than woman; the leopard is less savage and shameless.

*Chorus of Women.* And yet you dare to make war upon me, wretch, when you might have me for your most faithful friend and ally.

*Chorus of Old Men.* Never, never can my hatred cease towards women.

*Chorus of Women.* Well, please yourself. Still I cannot bear to leave you all naked as you are; folks would laugh at you. Come, I am going to put this tunic on you.

*Chorus of Old Men.* You are right, upon my word! it was only in my confounded fit of rage I took it off.

*Chorus of Women.* Now at any rate you look like a man, and they won't make fun of you. Ah! if you had not offended me so badly, I would take out that nasty insect you have in your eye for you.

*Chorus of Old Men.* Ah! so that's what was annoying me so! Look, here's a ring, just remove the insect, and show it me. By Zeus! it has been hurting my eye this ever so long.

*Chorus of Women.* Well, I agree, though your manners are not over and above pleasant. Oh! what a huge great gnat! just look! It's from Tricorysus, for sure.

*Chorus of Old Men.* A thousand thanks! the creature was digging a regular well in my eye; now it's gone, my tears flow freely.

*Chorus of Women.* I will wipe them for you—bad, naughty man though you are. Now, just one kiss.

*Chorus of Old Men.* No—a kiss, certainly not!

*Chorus of Women.* Just one, whether you like it or not.

*Chorus of Old Men.* Oh! those confounded women! how they do cajole us! How true the saying: " 'Tis impossible to live with the baggages, impossible to live without 'em!" Come, let us agree for the future not to regard each other any more as enemies; and to clinch the bargain, let us sing a choric song.

*Chorus of Women.* We desire, Athenians, to speak ill of no man; but on the contrary to say much good of everyone, and to *do* the like. We have had enough of misfortunes, and calamities. Is there any, man or woman, wants a bit of money—two or three minas or so; well, our purse is full. If only peace is concluded, the borrower will not have to pay back. Also I'm inviting to supper a few Carystian friends, who are excellently well qualified. I have still a drop of good soup left, and a young porker I'm going to kill, and the flesh will be sweet and tender. I shall expect you at my house to-day; but first away to the baths with you, you and your children; then come all of you, ask no one's leave, but walk straight up, as if you were at home; never fear, the door will be . . . shut in your faces!

*Chorus of Old Men.* Ah! here come the Envoys from Sparta with their long flowing beards; why, you would think they wore a cage between their thighs. (*Enter the Lacedoemonian Envoys.*) Hail to you, first of all, Laconians; then tell us how you fare.

*A Laconian.* No need for many words; you see what a state we are in.

*Chorus of Old Men.* Alas! the situation grows more and

more strained! the intensity of the thing is just frightful.

*Laconian.* 'Tis beyond belief! But to work! summon your Commissioners, and let us patch up the best peace we may.

*Chorus of Old Men.* Ah! our men too, like wrestlers in the arena, cannot endure a rag over their bellies; 'tis an athlete's malady, which only exercise can remedy.

*An Athenian.* Can anybody tell us where Lysistrata is? Surely she will have some compassion on our condition.

*Chorus of Old Men.* Look! 'tis the very same complaint. (*Addressing the Athenian.*) Don't you feel of mornings a strong nervous tension?

*Athenian.* Yes, and a dreadful, dreadful torture it is! Unless peace is made very soon, we shall find no recourse but go to Cleisthenes.

*Chorus of Old Men.* Take my advice, and put on your clothes again; one of the fellows who mutilated the Hermae might see you.

*Athenian.* You are right.

*Laconian.* Quite right. There, I will slip on my tunic.

*Athenian.* Oh! what a terrible state we are in! Greeting to you, Laconian fellow-sufferers.

*Laconian* (*addressing one of his countrymen*). Ah! my boy, what a thing it would have been if these fellows had seen us just now when we were on full stand!

*Athenian.* Speak out, Laconians, what is it brings you here?

*Laconian.* We have come to treat for peace.

*Athenian.* Well said; we are of the same mind. Better call Lysistrata then; she is the only person will bring us to terms.

*Laconian.* Yes, yes—and Lysistrata into the bargain, if you will.

*Chorus of Old Men.* Needless to call her; she has heard your voices, and here she comes.

*Athenian.* Hail, boldest and brávest of womankind! The

time is come to show yourself in turn uncompromising and conciliatory, exacting and yielding, haughty and condescending. Call up all your skill and artfulness. Lo! the foremost men in Hellas, seduced by your fascinations, are agreed to entrust you with the task of ending their quarrels.

*Lysistrata.* 'Twill be an easy task—if only they refrain from mutual indulgence in masculine love; if they do, I shall know the fact at once. Now, where is the gentle goddess Peace? Lead hither the Laconian Envoys. But, look you, no roughness or violence; our husbands always behaved so boorishly. Bring them to me with smiles, as women should. If any refuse to give you his hand, then catch him and draw him politely forward. Bring up the Athenians too; you may take them just how you will. Laconians, approach; and you, Athenians, on my other side. Now hearken all! I am but a woman; but I have good common sense; Nature has dowered me with discriminating judgment, which I have yet further developed, thanks to the wise teachings of my father and the elders of the city. First I must bring a reproach against you that applies equally to both sides. At Olympia, and Thermopylae, and Delphi, and a score of other places too numerous to mention, you celebrate before the same altars ceremonies common to all Hellenes; yet you go cutting each other's throats, and sacking Hellenic cities, when all the while the Barbarian is yonder threatening you! That is my first point.

*Athenian.* Ah, ah! concupiscence is killing me!

*Lysistrata.* Now 'tis to you I address myself, Laconians. Have you forgotten how Periclides, your own countryman, sat a suppliant before our altars? How pale he was in his purple robes! He had come to crave an army of us; 'twas the time when Messenia was pressing you sore, and the Sea-god was shaking the earth. Cimon marched to

your aid at the head of four thousand hoplites, and saved
Lacedaemon. And, after such a service as that, you ravage
the soil of your benefactors!

*Athenian.* They do wrong, very wrong, Lysistrata.

*Laconian.* We do wrong, very wrong. Ah! great gods!
what lovely thighs she has!

*Lysistrata.* And now a word to the Athenians. Have you
no memory left of how, in the days when ye wore the
tunic of slaves, the Laconians came, spear in hand, and
slew a host of Thessalians and partisans of Hippias the
Tyrant? They, and they only, fought on your side on that
eventful day; they delivered you from despotism, and
thanks to them our Nation could change the short tunic of
the slave for the long cloak of the free man.

*Laconian.* I have never seen a woman of more gracious
dignity.

*Athenian.* I have never seen a woman with a finer
body!

*Lysistrata.* Bound by such ties of mutual kindness, how
can you bear to be at war? Stop, stay the hateful strife,
be reconciled; what hinders you?

*Laconian.* We are quite ready, if they will give us back
our rampart.

*Lysistrata.* What rampart, my dear man?

*Laconian.* Pylos, which we have been asking for and
craving for ever so long.

*Athenian.* In the Sea-god's name, you shall never have
it!

*Lysistrata.* Agree, my friends, agree.

*Athenian.* But then what city shall we be able to stir up
trouble in?

*Lysistrata.* Ask for another place in exchange.

*Athenian.* Ah, that's the ticket! Well, to begin with,
give us Echinus, the Maliac gulf adjoining, and the two
legs of Megara.

*Laconian.* Oh! surely, surely not all that, my dear sir.

*Lysistrata.* Come to terms; never make a difficulty of two legs more or less!

*Athenian.* Well, I'm ready now to off coat and cultivate my land.

*Laconian.* And I too, to dung it to start with.

*Lysistrata.* That's just what you shall do, once peace is signed. So, if you really want to make it, go consult your allies about the matter.

*Athenian.* What allies, I should like to know? Why, we are *all* on the stand; not one but is mad to be mating. What we all want, is to be abed with our wives; how should our allies fail to second our project?

*Laconian.* And ours the same, for certain sure!

*Athenian.* The Carystians first and foremost, by the gods! .

*Lysistrata.* Well said, indeed! Now be off to purify yourselves for entering the Acropolis, where the women invite you to supper; we will empty our provision baskets to do you honour. At table, you will exchange oaths and pledges; then each man will go home with his wife.

*Athenian.* Come along then, and as quick as may be.

*Laconian.* Lead on; I'm your man.

*Athenian.* Quick, quick's the word, say I.

*Chorus of Women.* Embroidered stuffs, and dainty tunics, and flowing gowns, and golden ornaments, everything I have, I offer them you with all my heart; take them all for your children, for your girls, against they are chosen "basket-bearers" to the goddess. I invite you every one to enter, come in and choose whatever you will; there is nothing so well fastened, you cannot break the seals, and carry away the contents. Look about you everywhere . . . you won't find a blessed thing, unless you have sharper eyes than mine. And if any of you lacks corn to feed his slaves and his young and numerous family, why, I have a few grains of wheat at home; let him take what I have to give, a big twelve-pound loaf included. So let my poorer neighbours all come with bags and wallets; my man, Manes, shall give them corn; but I warn them not to come near my door, or—beware the dog!

*A Market-Lounger.* I say, you, open the door!

*A Slave.* Go your way, I tell you. Why, bless me, they're sitting down now; I shall have to singe 'em with my torch to make 'em stir! What an impudent lot of fellows!

*Market-Lounger.* I don't mean to budge.

*Slave.* Well, as you *must* stop, and I don't want to offend you—but you'll see some queer sights.

*Market-Lounger.* Well and good, I've no objection.

*Slave.* No, no, you must be off—or I'll tear your hair out, I will; be off, I say, and don't annoy the Laconian Envoys; they're just coming out from the banquet-hall.

*An Athenian.* Such a merry banquet I've never seen before! The Laconians were simply charming. After the drink is in, why, we're all wise men, all. It's only natural, to be sure, for sober, we're all fools. Take my advice, my fellow-countrymen, our Envoys should always be drunk. We go to Sparta; we enter the city sober; why, we must be picking a quarrel directly. We don't understand what they say to us, we imagine a lot they don't say at all, and we report home all wrong, all topsy-turvy. But, look you, to-day it's quite different; we're enchanted whatever happens; instead of Clitagoras, they might sing us Telamon, and we should clap our hands just the same. A perjury or two into the bargain, la! what does that matter to merry companions in their cups?

*Slave.* But here they are back again! Will you begone, you loafing scoundrels.

*Lounger.* Ah ha! here's the company coming out already.

*A Laconian.* My dear, sweet friend, come, take your flute in hand; I would fain dance and sing my best in honour of the Athenians and our noble selves.

*An Athenian.* Yes, take your flute, i' the gods' name. What a delight to see him dance!

*Chorus of Laconians.* Oh, Mnemosyné! inspire these men, inspire my muse who knows our exploits and those of the Athenians. With what a godlike ardour did they swoop down at Artemisium on the ships of the Medes! What a glorious victory was that! For the soldiers of Leonidas, they were like fierce wild-boars whetting their tushes. The sweat ran down their faces, and drenched all their limbs, for verily the Persians were as many as the sands of the seashore. Oh! Artemis, huntress queen, whose arrows pierce the denizens of the woods, virgin goddess, be thou favourable to the Peace we here conclude; through thee may our hearts be long united! May this treaty draw close for ever the bonds of a happy friendship! No more wiles and stratagems! Aid us, oh! aid us, maiden huntress!

*Lysistrata.* All is for the best; and now, Laconians, take your wives away home with you, and you, Athenians, yours. May husband live happily with wife, and wife with husband. Dance, dance, to celebrate our bliss, and let us be heedful to avoid like mistakes for the future.

*Chorus of Athenians.* Appear, appear, dancers, and the Graces with you! Let us invoke, one and all, Artemis, and her heavenly brother, gracious Apollo, patron of the dance, and Dionysus, whose eye darts flame, as he steps forward surrounded by the Maenad maids, and Zeus, who wields the flashing lightning, and his august, thrice-blessed spouse, the Queen of Heaven! These let us invoke, and all the other gods, calling all the inhabitants of the skies to witness the noble Peace now concluded under the fond auspices of Aphrodité. Io Paean! Io Paean! dance, leap, as in honour of a victory won. Evoé! Evoé! And you, our Laconian guests, sing us a new and inspiring strain!

*Chorus of Laconians.* Leave once more, oh! leave once

more the noble height of Taygetus, oh! Muse of Lacedaemon, and join us in singing the praises of Apollo of Amyclae, and Athena of the Brazen House, and the gallant twin sons of Tyndarus, who practise arms on the banks of Eurotas river. Haste, haste hither with nimble-footed pace, let us sing Sparta, the city that delights in choruses divinely sweet and graceful dances, when our maidens bound lightly by the river side, like frolicsome fillies, beating the ground with rapid steps and shaking their long locks in the wind, as Bacchantes wave their wands in the wild revels of the Wine-god. At their head, oh! chaste and beauteous goddess, daughter of Latona, Artemis, do thou lead the song and dance. A fillet binding thy waving tresses, appear in thy loveliness; leap like a fawn, strike thy divine hands together to animate the dance, and aid us to renown the valiant goddess of battles, great Athené of the Brazen House!

## THE BIRDS

# THE BIRDS

## *Dramatis Personae*

EUELPIDES.
PISTHETAERUS.
EPOPS (the Hoopoe).
TROCHILUS, Servant to Epops.
PHOENICOPTERUS.
HERALDS.
A PRIEST.
A POET.
A PROPHET.
METON, a Geometrician.
A COMMISSIONER.
A DEALER IN DECREES.
IRIS.
A PARRICIDE.
CINESIAS, a Dithyrambic Bard.
AN INFORMER.
PROMETHEUS.
POSIDON.
TRIBALLUS.
HERACLES.
SERVANT OF PISTHETAERUS.
MESSENGERS.
CHORUS OF BIRDS.

SCENE: A wild, desolate tract of open country; broken
    rocks and brushwood occupy the centre of the
    stage.

# THE BIRDS

*Euelpides* (*to his jay*). Do you think I should walk straight for yon tree?

*Pisthetaerus* (*to his crow*). Cursed beast, what are you croaking to me? . . . to retrace my steps?

*Euelpides.* Why, you wretch, we are wandering at random, we are exerting ourselves only to return to the same spot; 'tis labour lost.

*Pisthetaerus.* To think that I should trust to this crow, which has made me cover more than a thousand furlongs!

*Euelpides.* And I to this jay, who has torn every nail from my fingers!

*Pisthetaerus.* If only I knew where we were. . . .

*Euelpides.* Could you find your country again from here?

*Pisthetaerus.* No, I feel quite sure I could not, any more than could Execestides find his.

*Euelpides.* Oh dear! oh dear!

*Pisthetaerus.* Aye, aye, my friend, 'tis indeed the road of "oh dears" we are following.

*Euelpides.* That Philocrates, the bird-seller, played us a scurvy trick, when he pretended these two guides could help us to find Tereus, the Epops, who is a bird, without being born of one. He has indeed sold us this jay, a true son of Tharelides, for an obolus, and this crow for three, but what can they do? Why, nothing whatever but bite and scratch!—What's the matter with you then, that you keep opening your beak? Do you want us to fling ourselves headlong down these rocks? There is no road that way.

*Pisthetaerus.* Not even the vestige of a track in any direction.

*Euelpides.* And what does the crow say about the road to follow?

*Pisthetaerus.* By Zeus, it no longer croaks the same thing it did.

*Euelpides.* And which way does it tell us to go now?

*Pisthetaerus.* It says that, by dint of gnawing, it will devour my fingers.

*Euelpides.* What misfortune is ours! we strain every nerve to get to the birds, do everything we can to that end, and we cannot find our way! Yes, spectators, our madness is quite different from that of Sacas. He is not a citizen, and would fain be one at any cost; we, on the contrary, born of an honourable tribe and family and living in the midst of our fellow-citizens, we have fled from our country as hard as ever we could go. 'Tis not that we hate it; we recognize it to be great and rich, likewise that everyone has the right to ruin himself; but the crickets only chirrup among the fig-trees for a month or two, whereas the Athenians spend their whole lives in chanting forth judgments from their law-courts. That is why we started off with a basket, a stew-pot and some myrtle boughs and have come to seek a quiet country in which to settle. We are going to Tereus, the Epops, to learn from him, whether, in his aerial flights, he has noticed some town of this kind.

*Pisthetaerus.* Here! look!

*Euelpides.* What's the matter?

*Pisthetaerus.* Why, the crow has been pointing me to something up there for some time now.

*Euelpides*. And the jay is also opening its beak and craning its neck to show me I know not what. Clearly, there are some birds about here. We shall soon know, if we kick up a noise to start them.

*Pisthetaerus*. Do you know what to do? Knock your leg against this rock.

*Euelpides*. And you your head to double the noise.

*Pisthetaerus*. Well, then, use a stone instead; take one and hammer with it.

*Euelpides*. Good idea! Ho there, within! Slave! slave!

*Pisthetaerus*. What's that, friend! You say, "slave," to summon Epops! 'Twould be much better to shout, "Epops, Epops!"

*Euelpides*. Well then, Epops! Must I knock again? Epops!

*Trochilus*. Who's there? Who calls my master?

*Euelpides*. Apollo the Deliverer! what an enormous beak!

*Trochilus*. Good god! they are bird-catchers.

*Euelpides*. The mere sight of him petrifies me with terror. What a horrible monster!

*Trochilus*. Woe to you!

*Euelpides*. But we are not men.

*Trochilus*. What are you, then?

*Euelpides*. I am the Fearling, an African bird.

*Trochilus*. You talk nonsense.

*Euelpides*. Well, then, just ask it of my feet.

*Trochilus*. And this other one, what bird is it?

*Pisthetaerus*. I? I am a Cackling, from the land of the pheasants.

*Euelpides*. But you yourself, in the name of the gods! what animal are you?

*Trochilus*. Why, I am a slave-bird.

*Euelpides*. Why, have you been conquered by a cock?

*Trochilus*. No, but when my master was turned into a

peewit, he begged me to become a bird too, to follow and to serve him.

*Euelpides.* Does a bird need a servant, then?

*Trochilus.* 'Tis no doubt because he was a man. At times he wants to eat a dish of loach from Phalerum; I seize my dish and fly to fetch him some. Again he wants some pea-soup; I seize a ladle and a pot and run to get it.

*Euelpides.* This is, then, truly a running-bird. Come, Trochilus, do us the kindness to call your master.

*Trochilus.* Why, he has just fallen asleep after a feed of myrtle-berries and a few grubs.

*Euelpides.* Never mind; wake him up.

*Trochilus.* I am certain he will be angry. However, I will wake him to please you.

*Pisthetaerus.* You cursed brute! why, I am almost dead with terror!

*Euelpides.* Oh! my god! 'twas sheer fear that made me lose my jay.

*Pisthetaerus.* Ah! you great coward! were you so frightened that you let go your jay?

*Euelpides.* And did you not lose your crow, when you fell sprawling on the ground? Pray tell me that.

*Pisthetaerus.* No, no.

*Euelpides.* Where is it, then?

*Pisthetaerus.* It has flown away.

*Euelpides.* Then you did not let it go! Oh! you brave fellow!

*Epops.* Open the forest, that I may go out!

*Euelpides.* By Heracles! what a creature! what plumage! What means this triple crest?

*Epops.* Who wants me?

*Euelpides.* The twelve great gods have used you ill, meseems.

*Epops.* Are you chaffing me about my feathers? I have been a man, strangers.

*Euelpides.* 'Tis not you we are jeering at.

*Epops.* At what, then?

*Euelpides.* Why, 'tis your beak that looks so odd to us.

*Epops.* This is how Sophocles outrages me in his tragedies. Know, I once was Tereus.

*Euelpides.* You were Tereus, and what are you now? a bird or a peacock?

*Epops.* I am a bird.

*Euelpides.* Then where are your feathers? For I don't see them.

*Epops.* They have fallen off.

*Euelpides.* Through illness?

*Epops.* No. All birds moult their feathers, you know, every winter, and others grow in their place. But tell me, who are you?

*Euelpides.* We? We are mortals.

*Epops.* From what country?

*Euelpides.* From the land of the beautiful galleys.

*Epops.* Are you dicasts?

*Euelpides.* No, if anything, we are anti-dicasts.

*Epops.* Is that kind of seed sown among you?

*Euelpides.* You have to look hard to find even a little in our fields.

*Epops.* What brings you here?

*Euelpides.* We wish to pay you a visit.

*Epops.* What for?

*Euelpides.* Because you formerly were a man, like we are, formerly you had debts, as we have, formerly you did not want to pay them, like ourselves; furthermore, being turned into a bird, you have when flying seen all lands and seas. Thus you have all human knowledge as well as that of birds. And hence we have come to you to beg you to direct us to some cosy town, in which one can repose as if on thick coverlets.

*Epops.* And are you looking for a greater city than Athens?

*Euelpides.* No, not a greater, but one more pleasant to dwell in.

*Epops.* Then you are looking for an aristocratic country.

*Euelpides.* I? Not at all! I hold the son of Scellias in horror.

*Epops.* But, after all, what sort of city would please you best?

*Euelpides.* A place where the following would be the most important business transacted.—Some friend would come knocking at the door quite early in the morning saying, "By Olympian Zeus, be at my house early, as soon as you have bathed, and bring your children too. I am giving a nuptial feast, so don't fail, or else don't cross my threshold when I am in distress."

*Epops.* Ah! that's what may be called being fond of hardships. And what say you?

*Pisthetaerus.* My tastes are similar.

*Epops.* And they are?

*Pisthetaerus.* I want a town where the father of a handsome lad will stop in the street and say to me reproachfully as if I had failed him, "Ah! Is this well done, Stilbonides! You met my son coming from the bath after the gymnasium and you neither spoke to him, nor embraced him, nor took him with you, nor ever once twitched his parts. Would anyone call you an old friend of mine?"

*Epops.* Ah! wag, I see you are fond of suffering. But there is a city of delights, such as you want. 'Tis on the Red Sea.

*Euelpides.* Oh, no. Not a sea-port, where some fine morning the Salaminian galley can appear, bringing a writ-server along. Have you no Greek town you can propose to us?

*Epops.* Why not choose Lepreum in Elis for your settlement?

*Euelpides.* By Zeus! I could not look at Lepreum without disgust, because of Melanthius.

*Epops.* Then, again, there is the Opuntian, where you could live.

*Euelpides.* I would not be Opuntian for a talent. But come, what is it like to live with the birds? You should know pretty well.

*Epops.* Why, 'tis not a disagreeable life. In the first place, one has no purse.

*Euelpides.* That does away with much roguery.

*Epops.* For food the gardens yield us white sesamé, myrtle-berries, poppies and mint.

*Euelpides.* Why, 'tis the life of the newly-wed indeed.

*Pisthetaerus.* Ha! I am beginning to see a great plan, which will transfer the supreme power of the birds, if you will but take my advice.

*Epops.* Take your advice? In what way?

*Pisthetaerus.* In what way? Well, firstly, do not fly in all directions with open beak; it is not dignified. Among us, when we see a thoughtless man, we ask, "What sort of bird is this?" and Teleas answers, "'Tis a man who has no brain, a bird that has lost his head, a creature you cannot catch, for it never remains in any one place."

*Epops.* By Zeus himself! your jest hits the mark. What then is to be done?

*Pisthetaerus.* Found a city.

*Epops.* We birds? But what sort of city should we build?

*Pisthetaerus.* Oh, really, really! 'tis spoken like a fool! Look down.

*Epops.* I am looking.

*Pisthetaerus.* Now look upwards.

*Epops.* I am looking.

*Pisthetaerus.* Turn your head round.

*Epops.* Ah! 'twill be pleasant for me, if I end in twisting my neck!

*Pisthetaerus.* What have you seen?

*Epops.* The clouds and the sky.

*Pisthetaerus.* Very well! is not this the pole of the birds then?

*Epops.* How their pole?

*Pisthetaerus.* Or, if you like it, the land. And since it turns and passes through the whole universe, it is called, 'pole.' If you build and fortify it, you will turn your pole into a fortified city. In this way you will reign over mankind as you do over the grasshoppers and cause the gods to die of rabid hunger.

*Epops.* How so?

*Pisthetaerus.* The air is 'twixt earth and heaven. When we want to go to Delphi, we ask the Boeotians for leave of passage; in the same way, when men sacrifice to the gods, unless the latter pay you tribute, you exercise the right of every nation towards strangers and don't allow the smoke of the sacrifices to pass through your city and territory.

*Epops.* By earth! by snares! by network! I never heard of anything more cleverly conceived; and, if the other birds approve, I am going to build the city along with you.

*Pisthetaerus.* Who will explain the matter to them?

*Epops.* You must yourself. Before I came they were quite ignorant, but since I have lived with them I have taught them to speak.

*Pisthetaerus.* But how can they be gathered together?

*Epops.* Easily. I will hasten down to the coppice to waken my dear Procné! as soon as they hear our voices, they will come to us hot wing.

*Pisthetaerus.* My dear bird, lose no time, I beg. Fly at once into the coppice and awaken Procné.

*Epops.* Chase off drowsy sleep, dear companion. Let the sacred hymn gush from thy divine throat in melodious

strains; roll forth in soft cadence your refreshing melodies
to bewail the fate of Itys, which has been the cause of so
many tears to us both. Your pure notes rise through the
thick leaves of the yew-tree right up to the throne of
Zeus, where Phoebus listens to you, Phoebus with his
golden hair. And his ivory lyre responds to your plaintive
accents; he gathers the choir of the gods and from their
immortal lips rushes a sacred chant of blessed voices.
(*The flute is played behind the scene.*)

*Pisthetaerus.* Oh! by Zeus! what a throat that little bird
possesses. He has filled the whole coppice with honey-
sweet melody!

*Euelpides.* Hush!

*Pisthetaerus.* What's the matter?

*Euelpides.* Will you keep silence?

*Pisthetaerus.* What for?

*Euelpides.* Epops is going to sing again.

*Epops* (*in the coppice*). Epopoi, poi, popoi, epopoi,
popoi, here, here, quick, quick, quick, my comrades in the
air; all you, who pillage the fertile lands of the husband-
men, the numberless tribes who gather and devour the
barley seeds, the swift flying race who sing so sweetly.
And you whose gentle twitter resounds through the
fields with the little cry of tio, tio, tio, tio, tio, tio, tio, tio;
and you who hop about the branches of the ivy in the
gardens; the mountain birds, who feed on the wild olive
berries or the arbutus, hurry to come at my call, trioto,
trioto, totobrix; you also, who snap up the sharp-stinging
gnats in the marshy vales, and you who dwell in the fine
plain of Marathon, all damp with dew, and you, the
francolin with speckled wings; you too, the halcyons, who
flit over the swelling waves of the sea, come hither to hear
the tidings; let all the tribes of long-necked birds as-
semble here; know that a clever old man has come to us,
bringing an entirely new idea and proposing great re-

forms. Let all come to the debate here, here, here, here. Torotorotorotorotix, kikkobau, kikkobau, torotorotorotoro-lililix.

*Pisthetaerus.* Can you see any bird?

*Euelpides.* By Phoebus, no! and yet I am straining my eyesight to scan the sky.

*Pisthetaerus.* 'Twas really not worth Epops' while to go and bury himself in the thicket like a plover when a-hatching.

*Phoenicopterus.* Torotina, torotina.

*Pisthetaerus.* Hold, friend, here is another bird.

*Euelpides.* I' faith, yes! 'tis a bird, but of what kind? Isn't it a peacock?

*Pisthetaerus.* Epops will tell us. What is this bird?

*Epops.* 'Tis not one of those you are used to seeing; 'tis a bird from the marshes.

*Pisthetaerus.* Oh! oh! but he is very handsome with his wings as crimson as flame.

*Epops.* Undoubtedly; indeed he is called flamingo.

*Euelpides.* Hi! I say! You!

*Pisthetaerus.* What are you shouting for?

*Euelpides.* Why, here's another bird.

*Pisthetaerus.* Aye, indeed; 'tis a foreign bird too. What is this bird from beyond the mountains with a look as solemn as it is stupid?

*Epops.* He is called the Mede.

*Pisthetaerus.* The Mede! But, by Heracles! how, if a Mede, has he flown here without a camel?

*Euelpides.* Here's another bird with a crest.

*Pisthetaerus.* Ah! that's curious. I say, Epops, you are not the only one of your kind then?

*Epops.* This bird is the son of Philocles, who is the son of Epops; so that, you see, I am his grandfather; just as one might say, Hipponicus, the son of Callias, who is the son of Hipponicus.

*Pisthetaerus.* Then this bird is Callias! Why, what a lot of his feathers he has lost!

*Epops.* That's because he is honest; so the informers set upon him and the women too pluck out his feathers.

*Pisthetaerus.* By Posidon, do you see that many-coloured bird? What is his name?

*Epops.* This one! 'Tis the glutton.

*Pisthetaerus.* Is there another glutton besides Cleonymus? But why, if he is Cleonymus, has he not thrown away his crest? But what is the meaning of all these crests? Have these birds come to contend for the double stadium prize?

*Epops.* They are like the Carians, who cling to the crests of their mountains for greater safety.

*Pisthetaerus.* Oh, Posidon! do you see what swarms of birds are gathering here?

*Euelpides.* By Phoebus! what a cloud! The entrance to the stage is no longer visible, so closely do they fly together.

*Pisthetaerus.* Here is the partridge.

*Euelpides.* Faith! there is the francolin.

*Pisthetaerus.* There is the poachard.

*Euelpides.* Here is the kingfisher. And over yonder?

*Epops.* 'Tis the barber.

*Euelpides.* What? a bird a barber?

*Pisthetaerus.* Why, Sporgilus is one. Here comes the owl.

*Euelpides.* And who is it brings an owl to Athens?

*Pisthetaerus.* Here is the magpie, the turtle-dove, the swallow, the horned owl, the buzzard, the pigeon, the falcon, the ring-dove, the cuckoo, the red-foot, the red-cap, the purple-cap, the kestrel, the diver, the ousel, the osprey, the woodpecker.

*Euelpides.* Oh! oh! what a lot of birds! what a quantity of blackbirds! how they scold, how they come rushing up!

What a noise! what a noise! Can they be bearing us ill-will? Oh! there! there! they are opening their beaks and staring at us.

*Pisthetaerus.* Why, so they are.

*Chorus.* Popopopopopopopoi. Where is he who called me? Where am I to find him?

*Epops.* I have been waiting for you this long while! I never fail in my word to my friends.

*Chorus.* Titititititititi. What good thing have you to tell me?

*Epops.* Something that concerns our common safety, and that is just as pleasant as it is to the purpose. Two men who are subtle reasoners, have come here to seek me.

*Chorus.* Where? What? What are you saying?

*Epops.* I say, two old men have come from the abode of men to propose a vast and splendid scheme to us.

*Chorus.* Oh! 'tis a horrible, unheard-of crime! What are you saying?

*Epops.* Nay! never let my words scare you.

*Chorus.* What have you done then?

*Epops.* I have welcomed two men, who wish to live with us.

*Chorus.* And you have dared to do that!

*Epops.* Aye, and am delighted at having done so.

*Chorus.* Where are they?

*Epops.* In your midst, as I am.

*Chorus.* Ah! ah! we are betrayed; 'tis sacrilege! Our friend, he who picked up corn-seeds in the same plains as ourselves, has violated our ancient laws; he has broken the oaths that bind all birds; he has laid a snare for me, he has handed us over to the attacks of that impious race which, throughout all time, has never ceased to war against us. As for this traitorous bird, we will decide his case later, but the two old men shall be punished forthwith; we are going to tear them to pieces.

*Pisthetaerus.* 'Tis all over with us.

*Euelpides.* You are the sole cause of all our trouble. Why did you bring me from down yonder?

*Pisthetaerus.* To have you with me.

*Euelpides.* Say rather to have me melt into tears.

*Pisthetaerus.* Go to! you are talking nonsense.

*Euelpides.* How so?

*Pisthetaerus.* How will you be able to cry when once your eyes are pecked out?

*Chorus.* Io! io! forward to the attack, throw yourselves upon the foe, spill his blood; take to your wings and surround them on all sides. Woe to them! let us get to work with our beaks, let us devour them. Nothing can save them from our wrath, neither the mountain forests, nor the clouds that float in the sky, nor the foaming deep. Come, peck, tear to ribbons. Where is the chief of the cohort? Let him engage the right wing.

*Euelpides.* This is the fatal moment. Where shall I fly to, unfortunate wretch that I am?

*Pisthetaerus.* Stay! stop here!

*Euelpides.* That they may tear me to pieces?

*Pisthetaerus.* And how do you think to escape them?

*Euelpides.* I don't know at all.

*Pisthetaerus.* Come, I will tell you. We must stop and fight them. Let us arm ourselves with these stew-pots.

*Euelpides.* Why with the stew-pots?

*Pisthetaerus.* The owl will not attack us.

*Euelpides.* But do you see all those hooked claws?

*Pisthetaerus.* Seize the spit and pierce the foe on your side.

*Euelpides.* And how about my eyes?

*Pisthetaerus.* Protect them with this dish or this vinegar-pot.

*Euelpides.* Oh! what cleverness! what inventive genius! You are a great general, even greater than Nicias, where stratagem is concerned.

*Chorus.* Forward, forward, charge with your beaks!

Come, no delay. Tear, pluck, strike, flay them, and first of all smash the stew-pot.

*Epops.* Oh, most cruel of all animals, why tear these two men to pieces, why kill them? What have they done to you? They belong to the same tribe, to the same family as my wife.

*Chorus.* Are wolves to be spared? Are they not our most mortal foes? So let us punish them.

*Epops.* If they are your foes by nature, they are your friends in heart, and they come here to give you useful advice.

*Chorus.* Advice or a useful word from their lips, from them, the enemies of my forebears!

*Epops.* The wise can often profit by the lessons of a foe, for caution is the mother of safety. 'Tis just such a thing as one will not learn from a friend and which an enemy compels you to know. To begin with, 'tis the foe and not the friend that taught cities to build high walls, to equip long vessels of war; and 'tis this knowledge that protects our children, our slaves and our wealth.

*Chorus.* Well then, I agree, let us first hear them, for 'tis best; one can even learn something in an enemy's school.

*Pisthetaerus.* Their wrath seems to cool. Draw back a little.

*Epops.* 'Tis only justice, and you will thank me later.

*Chorus.* Never have we opposed your advice up to now.

*Pisthetaerus.* They are in a more peaceful mood; put down your stew-pot and your two dishes; spit in hand, doing duty for a spear, let us mount guard inside the camp close to the pot and watch in our arsenal closely; for we must not fly.

*Euelpides.* You are right. But where shall we be buried, if we die?

*Pisthetaerus.* In the Ceramicus; for, to get a public funeral, we shall tell the Strategi that we fell at Orneae, fighting the country's foes.

*Chorus.* Return to your ranks and lay down your courage beside your wrath as the Hoplites do. Then let us ask these men who they are, whence they come, and with what intent. Here, Epops, answer me.

*Epops.* Are you calling me? What do you want of me?

*Chorus.* Who are they? From what country?

*Epops.* Strangers, who have come from Greece, the land of the wise.

*Chorus.* And what fate has led them hither to the land of the birds?

*Epops.* Their love for you and their wish to share your kind of life; to dwell and remain with you always.

*Chorus.* Indeed, and what are their plans?

*Epops.* They are wonderful, incredible, unheard of.

*Chorus.* Why, do they think to see some advantage that determines them to settle here? Are they hoping with our help to triumph over their foes or to be useful to their friends?

*Epops.* They speak of benefits so great it is impossible either to describe or conceive them; all shall be yours, all that we see here, there, above and below us; this they vouch for.

*Chorus.* Are they mad?

*Epops.* They are the sanest people in the world.

*Chorus.* Clever men?

*Epops.* The slyest of foxes, cleverness its very self, men of the world, cunning, the cream of knowing folk.

*Chorus.* Tell them to speak and speak quickly; why, as I listen to you, I am beside myself with delight.

*Epops.* Here, you there, take all these weapons and hang them up inside close to the fire, near the figure of the god who presides there and under his protection; as for you, address the birds, tell them why I have gathered them together.

*Pisthetaerus.* Not I, by Apollo, unless they agree with me as the little ape of an armourer agreed with his wife, not to bite me, nor pull me by the parts, nor shove things up my . . .

*Chorus.* You mean the . . . (*Puts finger to bottom.*) Oh! be quite at ease.

*Pisthetaerus.* No, I mean my eyes.

*Chorus.* Agreed.

*Pisthetaerus.* Swear it.

*Chorus.* I swear it and, if I keep my promise, let judges and spectators give me the victory unanimously.

*Pisthetaerus.* It is a bargain.

*Chorus.* And if I break my word, may I succeed by one vote only.

*Herald.* Hearken, ye people! Hoplites, pick up your weapons and return to your firesides; do not fail to read the decrees of dismissal we have posted.

*Chorus.* Man is a truly cunning creature, but nevertheless explain. Perhaps you are going to show me some good way to extend my power, some way that I have not had the wit to find out and which you have discovered. Speak! 'tis to your own interest as well as to mine, for if you secure me some advantage, I will surely share it with you. But what object can have induced you to come among us? Speak boldly, for I shall not break the truce,— until you have told us all.

*Pisthetaerus.* I am bursting with desire to speak; I have already mixed the dough of my address and nothing prevents me from kneading it. . . . Slave! bring the chaplet and water, which you must pour over my hands. Be quick!

*Euelpides.* Is it a question of feasting? What does it all mean?

*Pisthetaerus.* By Zeus, no! but I am hunting for fine, tasty words to break down the hardness of their hearts.— I grieve so much for you, who at one time were kings . . .

*Chorus.* We kings! Over whom?

*Pisthetaerus.* . . . of all that exists, firstly of me and of this man, even of Zeus himself. Your race is older than Saturn, the Titans and the Earth.

*Chorus.* What, older than the Earth!

*Pisthetaerus.* By Phoebus, yes.

*Chorus.* By Zeus, but I never knew that before!

*Pisthetaerus.* 'Tis because you are ignorant and heedless, and have never read your Aesop. 'Tis he who tells us that the lark was born before all other creatures, indeed before the Earth; his father died of sickness, but the earth did not exist then; he remained unburied for five days, when the bird in its dilemma decided, for want of a better place, to entomb his father in its own head.

*Euelpides.* So that the lark's father is buried at Cephalae.

*Epops.* Hence, if we existed before the Earth, before the gods, the kingship belongs to us by right of priority.

*Euelpides.* Undoubtedly, but sharpen your beak well; Zeus won't be in a hurry to hand over his sceptre to the woodpecker.

*Pisthetaerus.* It was not the gods, but the birds, who were formerly the masters and kings over men; of this I have a thousand proofs. First of all, I will point you to the cock, who governed the Persians before all other monarchs, before Darius and Megabyzus. 'Tis in memory of his reign that he is called the Persian bird.

*Euelpides.* For this reason also, even to-day, he alone of all the birds wears his tiara straight on his head, like the Great King.

*Pisthetaerus.* He was so strong, so great, so feared, that even now, on account of his ancient power, everyone jumps out of bed as soon as ever he crows at daybreak. Blacksmiths, potters, tanners, shoemakers, bathmen, corn-dealers, lyre-makers and armourers, all put on their shoes and go to work before it is daylight.

*Euelpides*. I can tell you something anent that. 'Twas the cock's fault that I lost a splendid tunic of Phrygian wool. I was at a feast in the town, given to celebrate the birth of a child; I had drunk pretty freely and had just fallen asleep, when a cock, I suppose in a greater hurry than the rest, began to crow. I thought it was dawn and set out for Alimos. I had hardly got beyond the walls, when a foot-pad struck me in the back with his bludgeon; down I went and wanted to shout, but he had already made off with my mantle.

*Pisthetaerus*. Formerly also the kite was ruler and king over the Greeks.

*Epops*. The Greeks?

*Pisthetaerus*. And when he was king, 'twas he who first taught them to fall on their knees before the kites.

*Euelpides*. By Zeus! 'tis what I did myself one day on seeing a kite; but at the moment I was on my knees, and leaning backwards with mouth agape, I bolted an obolus and was forced to carry my bag home empty.

*Pisthetaerus*. The cuckoo was king of Egypt and of the whole of Phoenicia. When he called out "cuckoo," all the Phoenicians hurried to the fields to reap their wheat and their barley.

*Euelpides*. Hence no doubt the proverb, "Cuckoo! cuckoo! go to the fields, ye circumcised."

*Pisthetaerus*. So powerful were the birds, that the kings of Grecian cities, Agamemnon, Menelaus, for instance, carried a bird on the tips of their sceptres, who had his share of all presents.

*Euelpides*. That I didn't know and was much astonished when I saw Priam come upon the stage in the tragedies with a bird, which kept watching Lysicrates to see if he got any present.

*Pisthetaerus*. But the strongest proof of all is, that Zeus, who now reigns, is represented as standing with an eagle on his head as a symbol of his royalty; his daughter has an owl, and Phoebus, as his servant, has a hawk.

*Euelpides.* By Demeter, 'tis well spoken. But what are all these birds doing in heaven?

*Pisthetaerus.* When anyone sacrifices and, according to the rite, offers the entrails to the gods, these birds take their share before Zeus. Formerly men always swore by the birds and never by the gods; even now Lampon swears by the goose, when he wants to lie. . . . Thus 'tis clear that you were great and sacred, but now you are looked upon as slaves, as fools, as Helots; stones are thrown at you as at raving madmen, even in holy places. A crowd of bird-catchers sets snares, traps, limed-twigs and nets of all sorts for you; you are caught, you are sold in heaps and the buyers finger you over to be certain you are fat. Again, if they would but serve you up simply roasted; but they rasp cheese into a mixture of oil, vinegar and laserwort, to which another sweet and greasy sauce is added, and the whole is poured scalding hot over your back, for all the world as if you were diseased meat.

*Chorus.* Man, your words have made my heart bleed; I have groaned over the treachery of our fathers, who knew not how to transmit to us the high rank they held from their forefathers. But 'tis a benevolent Genius, a happy Fate, that sends you to us; you shall be our deliverer and I place the destiny of my little ones and my own in your hands with every confidence. But hasten to tell me what must be done; we should not be worthy to live, if we did not seek to regain our royalty by every possible means.

*Pisthetaerus.* First I advise that the birds gather together in one city and that they build a wall of great bricks, like that at Babylon, round the plains of the air and the whole region of space that divides earth from heaven.

*Epops.* Oh, Cebriones! oh, Porphyrion! what a terribly strong place!

*Pisthetaerus.* This, this being well done and completed, you demand back the empire from Zeus; if he will not agree, if he refuses and does not at once confess himself beaten, you declare a sacred war against him and forbid the gods henceforward to pass through your country with lust, as hitherto, for the purpose of fondling their Alcmenas, their Alopés, or their Semelés! if they try to pass through, you infibulate them with rings so that they can work no longer. You send another messenger to mankind, who will proclaim to them that the birds are kings, that for the future they must first of all sacrifice to them, and only afterwards to the gods; that it is fitting to appoint to each deity the bird that has most in common with it. For instance, are they sacrificing to Aphrodité, let them at the same time offer barley to the coot; are they immolating a sheep to Posidon, let them consecrate wheat in honour of the duck; is a steer being offered to Heracles, let honey-cakes be dedicated to the gull; is a goat being slain for King Zeus, there is a King-Bird, the wren, to whom the sacrifice of a male gnat is due before Zeus himself even.

*Euelpides.* This notion of an immolated gnat delights me! And now let the great Zeus thunder!

*Epops.* But how will mankind recognize us as gods and not as jays? Us, who have wings and fly?

*Pisthetaerus.* You talk rubbish! Hermes is a god and has wings and flies, and so do many other gods. First of all, Victory flies with golden wings, Eros is undoubtedly winged too, and Iris is compared by Homer to a timorous dove. If men in their blindness do not recognize you as gods and continue to worship the dwellers in Olympus, then a cloud of sparrows greedy for corn must descend upon their fields and eat up all their seeds; we shall see then if Demeter will mete them out any wheat.

*Euelpides.* By Zeus, she'll take good care she does not, and you will see her inventing a thousand excuses.

*Pisthetaerus.* The crows too will prove your divinity to them by pecking out the eyes of their flocks and of their draught-oxen; and then let Apollo cure them, since he is a physician and is paid for the purpose.

*Euelpides.* Oh! don't do that! Wait first until I have sold my two young bullocks.

*Pisthetaerus.* If on the other hand they recognize that you are God, the principle of life, that you are Earth, Saturn, Posidon, they shall be loaded with benefits.

*Epops.* Name me one of these then.

*Pisthetaerus.* Firstly, the locusts shall not eat up their vine-blossoms; a legion of owls and kestrels will devour them. Moreover, the gnats and the gall-bugs shall no longer ravage the figs; a flock of thrushes shall swallow the whole host down to the very last.

*Epops.* And how shall we give wealth to mankind? This is their strongest passion.

*Pisthetaerus.* When they consult the omens, you will point them to the richest mines, you will reveal the paying ventures to the diviner, and not another shipwreck will happen or sailor perish.

*Epops.* No more shall perish? How is that?

*Pisthetaerus.* When the auguries are examined before starting on a voyage, some bird will not fail to say, "Don't start! there will be a storm," or else, "Go! you will make a most profitable venture."

*Euelpides.* I shall buy a trading-vessel and go to sea. I will not stay with you.

*Pisthetaerus.* You will discover treasures to them, which were buried in former times, for you know them. Do not all men say, "None know where my treasure lies, unless perchance it be some bird."

*Euelpides.* I shall sell my boat and buy a spade to unearth the vessels.

*Epops.* And how are we to give them health, which belongs to the gods?

*Pisthetaerus.* If they are happy, is not that the chief thing towards health? The miserable man is never well.

*Epops.* Old Age also dwells in Olympus. How will they get at it? Must they die in early youth?

*Pisthetaerus.* Why, the birds, by Zeus, will add three hundred years to their life.

*Epops.* From whom will they take them?

*Pisthetaerus.* From whom? Why, from themselves. Don't you know the cawing crow lives five times as long as a man?

*Euelpides.* Ah! ah! these are far better kings for us than Zeus!

*Pisthetaerus.* Far better, are they not? And firstly, we shall not have to build them temples of hewn stone, closed with gates of gold; they will dwell amongst the bushes and in the thickets of green oak; the most venerated of birds will have no other temple than the foliage of the olive tree; we shall not go to Delphi or to Ammon to sacrifice; but standing erect in the midst of arbutus and wild olives and holding forth our hands filled with wheat and barley, we shall pray them to admit us to a share of the blessings they enjoy and shall at once obtain them for a few grains of wheat.

*Chorus.* Old man, whom I detested, you are now to me the dearest of all; never shall I, if I can help it, fail to follow your advice. Inspirited by your words, I threaten my rivals the gods, and I swear that if you march in alliance with me against the gods and are faithful to our just, loyal and sacred bond, we shall soon have shattered their sceptre. 'Tis our part to undertake the toil, 'tis yours to advise.

*Epops.* By Zeus! 'tis no longer the time to delay and loiter like Nicias; let us act as promptly as possible. . . .

In the first place, come, enter my nest built of brushwood and blades of straw, and tell me your names.

*Pisthetaerus.* That is soon done; my name is Pisthetaerus.

*Epops.* And his?

*Pisthetaerus.* Euelpides, of the deme of Thria.

*Epops.* Good! and good luck to you.

*Pisthetaerus.* We accept the omen.

*Epops.* Come in here.

*Pisthetaerus.* Very well, 'tis you who lead us and must introduce us.

*Epops.* Come then.

*Pisthetaerus.* Oh! my god! do come back here. Hi! tell us how we are to follow you. You can fly, but we cannot.

*Epops.* Well, well.

*Pisthetaerus.* Remember Aesop's fables. It is told there, that the fox fared very ill, because he had made an alliance with the eagle.

*Epops.* Be at ease. You shall eat a certain root and wings will grow on your shoulders.

*Pisthetaerus.* Then let us enter. Xanthias and Manes, pick up our baggage.

*Chorus.* Hi! Epops! do you hear me?

*Epops.* What's the matter?

*Chorus.* Take them off to dine well and call your mate, the melodious Procné, whose songs are worthy of the Muses; she will delight our leisure moments.

*Pisthetaerus.* Oh! I conjure you, accede to their wish; for this delightful bird will leave her rushes at the sound of your voice; for the sake of the gods, let her come here, so that we may contemplate the nightingale.

*Epops.* Let it be as you desire. Come forth, Procné, show yourself to these strangers.

*Pisthetaerus.* Oh! great Zeus! what a beautiful little bird! what a dainty form! what brilliant plumage!

*Euelpides.* Do you know how dearly I should like to split her legs for her?

*Pisthetaerus.* She is dazzling all over with gold, like a young girl.

*Euelpides.* Oh! how I should like to kiss her!

*Pisthetaerus.* Why, wretched man, she has two little sharp points on her beak.

*Euelpides.* I would treat her like an egg, the shell of which we remove before eating it; I would take off her mask and then kiss her pretty face.

*Epops.* Let us go in.

*Pisthetaerus.* Lead the way, and may success attend us.

*Chorus.* Lovable golden bird, whom I cherish above all others, you, whom I associate with all my songs, nightingale, you have come, you have come, to show yourself to me and to charm me with your notes. Come, you, who play spring melodies upon the harmonious flute, lead off our anapaests.

Weak mortals, chained to the earth, creatures of clay as frail as the foliage of the woods, you unfortunate race, whose life is but darkness, as unreal as a shadow, the illusion of a dream, hearken to us, who are immortal beings, ethereal, ever young and occupied with eternal thoughts, for we shall teach you about all celestial matters; you shall know thoroughly what is the nature of the birds, what the origin of the gods, of the rivers, of Erebus, and Chaos; thanks to us, Prodicus will envy you your knowledge.

At the beginning there was only Chaos, Night, dark Erebus, and deep Tartarus. Earth, the air and heaven had no existence. Firstly, black-winged Night laid a germless egg in the bosom of the infinite deeps of Erebus, and from this, after the revolution of long ages, sprang the graceful Eros with his glittering golden wings, swift as the whirlwinds of the tempest. He mated in deep Tartarus with dark Chaos, winged like himself, and thus hatched forth our race, which was the first to see the light. That of the Immortals did not exist until Eros had brought together all the ingredients of the world, and from their marriage Heaven, Ocean, Earth and the imperishable race of blessed gods sprang into being. Thus our origin is very much older than that of the dwellers in Olympus. We are the offspring of Eros; there are a thousand proofs to show it. We have wings and we lend assistance to lovers. How many handsome youths, who had sworn to remain insensible, have not been vanquished by our power and have yielded themselves to their lovers when almost at the end of their youth, being led away by the gift of a quail, a waterfowl, a goose, or a cock.

And what important services do not the birds render to mortals! First of all, they mark the seasons for them, springtime, winter, and autumn. Does the screaming crane migrate to Libya,—it warns the husbandman to sow, the pilot to take his ease beside his tiller hung up in his dwelling, and Orestes to weave a tunic, so that the rigorous cold may not drive him any more to strip other folk. When the kite reappears, he tells of the return of spring and of the period when the fleece of the sheep must be clipped. Is the swallow in sight? All hasten to sell their warm tunic and to buy some light clothing. We are your Ammon, Delphi, Dodona, your Phoebus Apollo. Before undertaking anything, whether a business transaction, a marriage, or the purchase of food, you consult the birds by reading the omens, and you give this name of omen to all signs that tell of the future. With you a word is an omen, you call a sneeze an omen, a meeting an omen, an unknown sound an omen, a slave or an ass an omen. Is it not clear that we are a prophetic Apollo to you? If you recognize us as gods, we shall be your divining Muses, through us you will know the winds and the seasons, summer, winter, and the temperate months.

We shall not withdraw ourselves to the highest clouds like Zeus, but shall be among you and shall give to you and to your children and the children of your children, health and wealth, long life, peace, youth, laughter, songs and feasts; in short, you will all be so well off, that you will be weary and satiated with enjoyment.

Oh, rustic Muse of such varied note, tio, tio, tio, tiotinx, I sing with you in the groves and on the mountain tops, tio, tio, tio, tio, tiotinx. I pour forth sacred strains from my golden throat in honour of the god Pan, tio, tio, tio, tiotinx, from the top of the thickly leaved ash, and my voice mingles with the mighty choirs who extol Cybelé on the mountain tops, totototototototinx. 'Tis to our concerts that Phrynichus comes to pillage like a bee the ambrosia of his songs, the sweetness of which so charms the ear, tio, tio, tio, tio, tinx.

If there be one of you spectators who wishes to spend the rest of his life quietly among the birds, let him come to us. All that is disgraceful and forbidden by law on earth is on the contrary honourable among us, the birds. For instance, among you 'tis a crime to beat your father, but with us 'tis an estimable deed; it's considered fine to run straight at your father and hit him, saying, "Come, lift your spur if you want to fight." The runaway slave, whom you brand, is only a spotted francolin with us. Are you Phrygian like Spintharus? Among us you would be the Phrygian bird, the goldfinch, of the race of Philemon. Are you a slave and a Carian like Execestides? Among us you can create yourself forefathers; you can always find relations. Does the son of Pisias want to betray the gates of the city to the foe? Let him become a partridge, the fitting offspring of his father; among us there is no shame in escaping as cleverly as a partridge.

So the swans on the banks of the Hebrus, tio, tio, tio, tio, tiotinx, mingle their voices to serenade Apollo, tio, tio, tio, tio, tiotinx, flapping their wings the while, tio,

tio, tio, tio, tiotinx; their notes reach beyond the clouds
of heaven; all the dwellers in the forests stand still with
astonishment and delight; a calm rests upon the waters,
and the Graces and the choirs in Olympus catch up the
strain, tio, tio, tio, tio, tiotinx.

There is nothing more useful nor more pleasant than
to have wings. To begin with, just let us suppose a spectator to be dying with hunger and to be weary of the
choruses of the tragic poets; if he were winged, he would
fly off, go home to dine and come back with his stomach
filled. Some Patroclides in urgent need would not have to
soil his cloak, but could fly off, satisfy his requirements,
and, having recovered his breath, return. If one of you,
it matters not who, had adulterous relations and saw the
husband of his mistress in the seats of the senators, he
might stretch his wings, fly thither, and, having appeased
his craving, resume his place. Is it not the most priceless
gift of all, to be winged? Look at Diitrephes! His wings
were only wickerwork ones, and yet he got himself
chosen Phylarch and then Hipparch; from being nobody,
he has risen to be famous; 'tis now the finest gilded cock
of his tribe.

*Pisthetaerus.* Halloa! What's this? By Zeus! I never saw
anything so funny in all my life.

*Euelpides.* What makes you laugh?

*Pisthetaerus.* 'Tis your bits of wings. D'you know what
you look like? Like a goose painted by some dauber-fel-
low.

*Euelpides.* And you look like a close-shaven blackbird.

*Pisthetaerus.* 'Tis ourselves asked for this transforma-
tion, and, as Aeschylus has it, "These are no borrowed
feathers, but truly our own."

*Epops.* Come now, what must be done?

*Pisthetaerus.* First give our city a great and famous
name, then sacrifice to the gods.

*Euelpides.* I think so too.

*Epops.* Let's see. What shall our city be called?

*Pisthetaerus.* Will you have a high-sounding Laconian name? Shall we call it Sparta?

*Euelpides.* What! call my town Sparta? Why, I would not use esparto for my bed, even though I had nothing but bands of rushes.

*Pisthetaerus.* Well then, what name can you suggest?

*Euelpides.* Some name borrowed from the clouds, from these lofty regions in which we dwell—in short, some well-known name.

*Pisthetaerus.* Do you like Nephelococcygia?

*Epops.* Oh! capital! truly 'tis a brilliant thought!

*Euelpides.* Is it in Nephelococcygia that all the wealth of Theovenes and most of Aeschines' is?

*Pisthetaerus.* No, 'tis rather the plain of Phlegra, where the gods withered the pride of the sons of the Earth with their shafts.

*Euelpides.* Oh! what a splendid city! But what god shall be its patron? for whom shall we weave the peplus?

*Pisthetaerus.* Why not choose Athené Polias?

*Euelpides.* Oh! what a well-ordered town 'twould be to have a female deity armed from head to foot, while Cleisthenes was spinning!

*Pisthetaerus.* Who then shall guard the Pelargicon?

*Epops.* One of ourselves, a bird of Persian strain, who is everywhere proclaimed to be the bravest of all, a true chick of Ares.

*Euelpides.* Oh! noble chick! what a well-chosen god for a rocky home!

*Pisthetaerus.* Come! into the air with you to help the workers who are building the wall; carry up rubble, strip yourself to mix the mortar, take up the hod, tumble down the ladder, an you like, post sentinels, keep the fire smouldering beneath the ashes, go round the walls, bell in hand, and go to sleep up there yourself; then despatch two heralds, one to the gods above, the other to mankind on earth and come back here.

*Euelpides.* As for yourself, remain here, and may the plague take you for a troublesome fellow!

*Pisthetaerus.* Go, friend, go where I send you, for without you my orders cannot be obeyed. For myself, I want to sacrifice to the new god, and I am going to summon the priest who must preside at the ceremony. Slaves! Slaves! bring forward the basket and the lustral water.

*Chorus.* I do as you do, and I wish as you wish, and I implore you to address powerful and solemn prayers to the gods, and in addition to immolate a sheep as a token of our gratitude. Let us sing the Pythian chant in honour of the god, and let Chaeris accompany our voices.

*Pisthetaerus* (*to the flute-player*). Enough! but, by Heracles! what is this? Great gods! I have seen many prodigious things, but I never saw a muzzled raven.

*Epops.* Priest! 'tis high time! Sacrifice to the new gods.

*Priest.* I begin, but where is he with the basket? Pray to the Vesta of the birds, to the kite, who presides over the hearth, and to all the god and goddess-birds who dwell in Olympus.

*Chorus.* Oh! Hawk, the sacred guardian of Sunium, oh, god of the storks!

*Priest.* Pray to the swan of Delos, to Latona the mother of the quails, and to Artemis, the goldfinch.

*Pisthetaerus.* 'Tis no longer Artemis Colaenis, but Artemis the goldfinch.

*Priest.* And to Bacchus, the finch, and Cybelé, the ostrich and mother of the gods and mankind.

*Chorus.* Oh! sovereign ostrich, Cybelé, the mother of Cleocritus, grant health and safety to the Nephelococcygians as well as to the dwellers in Chios . . .

*Pisthetaerus.* The dwellers in Chios! Ah! I am delighted they should be thus mentioned on all occasions.

*Chorus.* . . . to the heroes, the birds, to the sons of heroes, to the porphyrion, the pelican, the spoon-bill, the redbreast, the grouse, the peacock, the horned-owl, the teal, the bittern, the heron, the stormy petrel, the fig-pecker, the titmouse . . .

*Pisthetaerus.* Stop! stop! you drive me crazy with your endless list. Why, wretch, to what sacred feast are you inviting the vultures and the sea-eagles? Don't you see that a single kite could easily carry off the lot at once? Begone, you and your fillets and all; I shall know how to complete the sacrifice by myself.

*Priest.* It is imperative that I sing another sacred chant for the rite of the lustral water, and that I invoke the immortals, or at least one of them, provided always that you have some suitable food to offer him; from what I see here, in the shape of gifts, there is naught whatever but horn and hair.

*Pisthetaerus.* Let us address our sacrifices and our prayers to the winged gods.

*A Poet.* Oh, Muse! celebrate happy Nephelococcygia in your hymns.

*Pisthetaerus.* What have we here? Where do you come from, tell me? Who are you?

*Poet.* I am he whose language is sweeter than honey, the zealous slave of the Muses, as Homer has it.

*Pisthetaerus.* You a slave! and yet you wear your hair long?

*Poet.* No, but the fact is all we poets are the assiduous slaves of the Muses, according to Homer.

*Pisthetaerus.* In truth your little cloak is quite holy too through zeal! But, poet, what ill wind drove you here?

*Poet.* I have composed verses in honour of your Nephelococcygia, a host of splendid dithyrambs and parthenians, worthy of Simonides himself.

*Pisthetaerus.* And when did you compose them? How long since?

*Poet.* Oh! 'tis long, aye, very long, that I have sung in honour of this city.

*Pisthetaerus.* But I am only celebrating its foundation with this sacrifice; I have only just named it, as is done with little babies.

*Poet.* "Just as the chargers fly with the speed of the wind, so does the voice of the Muses take its flight. Oh! thou noble founder of the town of Aetna, thou, whose name recalls the holy sacrifices, make us such gift as thy generous heart shall suggest."

*Pisthetaerus.* He will drive us silly if we do not get rid of him by some present. Here! you, who have a fur as well as your tunic, take it off and give it to this clever poet. Come, take this fur; you look to me to be shivering with cold.

*Poet.* My Muse will gladly accept this gift; but engrave these verses of Pindar's on your mind.

*Pisthetaerus.* Oh! what a pest! 'Tis impossible then to be rid of him.

*Poet.* "Straton wanders among the Scythian nomads, but has no linen garment. He is sad at only wearing an animal's pelt and no tunic." Do you conceive my bent?

*Pisthetaerus.* I understand that you want me to offer you a tunic. Hi! you (*to Euelpides*), take off yours; we must help the poet. . . . Come, you, take it and begone.

*Poet.* I am going, and these are the verses that I address to this city: "Phoebus of the golden throne, celebrate this shivery, freezing city; I have travelled through fruitful and snow-covered plains. Tralala! Tralala!"

*Pisthetaerus.* What are you chanting us about frosts? Thanks to the tunic, you no longer fear them. Ah! by Zeus! I could not have believed this cursed fellow could so soon have learnt the way to our city. Come, priest, take the lustral water and circle the altar.

*Priest.* Let all keep silence!

*A Prophet.* Let not the goat be sacrificed.

*Pisthetaerus.* Who are you?

*Prophet.* Who am I? A prophet.

*Pisthetaerus.* Get you gone.

*Prophet.* Wretched man, insult not sacred things. For there is an oracle of Bacis, which exactly applies to Nephelococcygia.

*Pisthetaerus.* Why did you not reveal it to me before I founded my city?

*Prophet.* The divine spirit was against it.

*Pisthetaerus.* Well, 'tis best to know the terms of the oracle.

*Prophet.* "But when the wolves and the white crows shall dwell together between Corinth and Sicyon. . . ."

*Pisthetaerus.* But how do the Corinthians concern me?

*Prophet.* 'Tis the regions of the air that Bacis indicated in this manner. "They must first sacrifice a white-fleeced goat to Pandora, and give the prophet, who first reveals my words, a good cloak and new sandals."

*Pisthetaerus.* Are the sandals there?

*Prophet.* Read. "And besides this a goblet of wine and a good share of the entrails of the victim."

*Pisthetaerus.* Of the entrails—is it so written?

*Prophet.* Read. "If you do as I command, divine youth, you shall be an eagle among the clouds; if not, you shall be neither turtle-dove, nor eagle, nor woodpecker."

*Pisthetaerus.* Is all that there?

*Prophet.* Read.

*Pisthetaerus.* This oracle in no sort of way resembles the one Apollo dictated to me: "If an impostor comes without invitation to annoy you during the sacrifice and to demand a share of the victim, apply a stout stick to his ribs."

*Prophet.* You are drivelling.

*Pisthetaerus.* "And don't spare him, were he an eagle from out of the clouds, were it Lampon himself or the great Diopithes."

*Prophet.* Is all that there?

*Pisthetaerus.* Here, read it yourself, and go and hang yourself.

*Chorus.* Oh! unfortunate wretch that I am.

*Pisthetaerus.* Away with you, and take your prophecies elsewhere.

*Meton.* I have come to you.

*Pisthetaerus.* Yet another pest. What have you come to do? What's your plan? What's the purpose of your journey? Why these splendid buskins?

*Meton.* I want to survey the plains of the air for you and to parcel them into lots.

*Pisthetaerus.* In the name of the gods, who are you?

*Meton.* Who am I? Meton, known throughout Greece and at Colonus.

*Pisthetaerus.* What are these things?

*Meton.* Tools for measuring the air. In truth, the spaces in the air have precisely the form of a furnace. With this bent ruler I draw a line from top to bottom; from one of its points I describe a circle with the compass. Do you understand?

*Pisthetaerus.* Not the very least.

*Meton.* With the straight ruler I set to work to inscribe a square within this circle; in its centre will be the market-place, into which all the straight streets will lead, converging to this centre like a star, which, although only orbicular, sends forth its rays in a straight line from all sides.

*Pisthetaerus.* Meton, you new Thales.

*Meton.* What d'you want with me?

*Pisthetaerus.* I want to give you a proof of my friendship. Use your legs.

*Meton.* Why, what have I to fear?

*Pisthetaerus.* 'Tis the same here as in Sparta. Strangers are driven away, and blows rain down as thick as hail.

*Meton.* Is there sedition in your city?

*Pisthetaerus.* No, certainly not.

*Meton.* What's wrong then?

*Pisthetaerus.* We are agreed to sweep all quacks and impostors far from our borders.

*Meton.* Then I'm off.

*Pisthetaerus.* I fear me 'tis too late. The thunder growls already. (*Beats him.*)

*Meton.* Oh, woe! oh, woe!

*Pisthetaerus.* I warned you. Now, be off, and do your surveying somewhere else. (*Meton takes to his heels.*)

*An Inspector.* Where are the Proxeni?

*Pisthetaerus.* Who is this Sardanapalus?

*Inspector.* I have been appointed by lot to come to Nephelococcygia as inspector.

*Pisthetaerus.* An inspector! and who sends you here, you rascal?

*Inspector.* A decree of Taleas.

*Pisthetaerus.* Will you just pocket your salary, do nothing, and be off?

*Inspector.* I' faith! that I will; I am urgently needed to be at Athens to attend the assembly; for I am charged with the interests of Pharnaces.

*Pisthetaerus.* Take it then, and be off. See, here is your salary. (*Beats him.*)

*Inspector.* What does this mean?

*Pisthetaerus.* 'Tis the assembly where you have to defend Pharnaces.

*Inspector.* You shall testify that they dare to strike me, the inspector.

*Pisthetaerus.* Are you not going to clear out with your urns? 'Tis not to be believed; they send us inspectors before we have so much as paid sacrifice to the gods.

*A Dealer in Decrees.* "If the Nephelococcygian does wrong to the Athenian . . ."

*Pisthetaerus.* Now whatever are these cursed parchments?

*Dealer in Decrees.* I am a dealer in decrees, and I have come here to sell you the new laws.

*Pisthetaerus.* Which?

*Dealer in Decrees.* "The Nephelococcygians shall adopt the same weights, measures and decrees as the Olophyxians."

*Pisthetaerus.* And you shall soon be imitating the Ototyxians. (*Beats him.*)

*Dealer in Decrees.* Hullo! what are you doing?

*Pisthetaerus.* Now will you be off with your decrees? For I am going to let *you* see some severe ones.

*Inspector (returning).* I summon Pisthetaerus for outrage for the month of Munychion.

*Pisthetaerus.* Ha! my friend! are you still there?

*Dealer in Decrees.* "Should anyone drive away the magistrates and not receive them, according to the decree duly posted . . ."

*Pisthetaerus.* What! rascal! you are there too?

*Inspector.* Woe to you! I'll have you condemned to a fine of ten thousand drachmae.

*Pisthetaerus.* And I'll smash your urns.

*Inspector.* Do you recall that evening when you stooled against the column where the decrees are posted?

*Pisthetaerus.* Here! here! let him be seized. (*The inspector runs off.*) Well! don't you want to stop any longer?

*Priest.* Let us get indoors as quick as possible; we will sacrifice the goat inside.

*Chorus.* Henceforth it is to me that mortals must address their sacrifices and their prayers. Nothing escapes my sight nor my might. My glance embraces the universe, I preserve the fruit in the flower by destroying the thousand kinds of voracious insects the soil produces, which attack the trees and feed on the germ when it has scarcely formed in the calyx; I destroy those who ravage the balmy terrace gardens like a deadly plague; all these

95

gnawing crawling creatures perish beneath the lash of my wing. I hear it proclaimed everywhere: "A talent for him who shall kill Diagoras of Melos, and a talent for him who destroys one of the dead tyrants." We likewise wish to make our proclamation: "A talent to him among you who shall kill Philocrates, the Strouthian; four, if he brings him to us alive. For this Philocrates skewers the finches together and sells them at the rate of an obolus for seven. He tortures the thrushes by blowing them out, so that they may look bigger, sticks their own feathers into the nostrils of blackbirds, and collects pigeons, which he shuts up and forces them, fastened in a net, to decoy others." That is what we wish to proclaim. And if anyone is keeping birds shut up in his yard, let him hasten to let them loose; those who disobey shall be seized by the birds and we shall put them in chains, so that in their turn they may decoy other men.

Happy indeed is the race of winged birds who need no cloak in winter! Neither do I fear the relentless rays of the fiery dog-days; when the divine grasshopper, intoxicated with the sunlight, when noon is burning the ground, is breaking out into shrill melody, my home is beneath the foliage in the flowery meadows. I winter in deep caverns, where I frolic with the mountain nymphs, while in spring I despoil the gardens of the Graces and gather the white, virgin berry on the myrtle bushes. I want now to speak to the judges about the prize they are going to award; if they are favourable to us, we will load them with benefits far greater than those Paris received. Firstly, the owls of Laurium, which every judge desires above all things, shall never be wanting to you; you shall see them homing with you, building their nests in your money-bags and laying coins. Besides, you shall be housed like the gods, for we shall erect gables over your dwellings; if you hold some public post and want to do a little pilfering, we will give you the sharp claws of a hawk. Are you dining in town, we will provide you with crops. But, if your award is against us, don't fail to have metal covers fashioned for yourselves, like those they place over statues; else, look out! for the day you wear a white tunic all the birds will soil it with their droppings.

*Pisthetaerus.* Birds! the sacrifice is propitious. But I see no messenger coming from the wall to tell us what is happening. Ah! here comes one running himself out of breath as though he were running the Olympic stadium.

*Messenger.* Where, where is he? Where, where, where is he? Where, where, where is he? Where is Pisthetaerus, our leader?

*Pisthetaerus.* Here am I.

*Messenger.* The wall is finished.

*Pisthetaerus.* That's good news.

*Messenger.* 'Tis a most beautiful, a most magnificent work of art. The wall is so broad, that Proxenides, the Braggartian, and Theogenes could pass each other in their chariots, even if they were drawn by steeds as big as the Trojan horse.

*Pisthetaerus.* 'Tis wonderful!

*Messenger.* Its length is one hundred stadia; I measured it myself.

*Pisthetaerus.* A decent length, by Posidon! And who built such a wall?

*Messenger.* Birds—birds only; they had neither Egyptian brickmaker, nor stonemason, nor carpenter; the birds did it all themselves; I could hardly believe my eyes. Thirty thousand cranes came from Libya with a supply of stones, intended for the foundations. The water-rails chiselled them with their beaks. Ten thousand storks were busy making bricks; plovers and other water fowl carried water into the air.

*Pisthetaerus.* And who carried the mortar?

*Messenger.* Herons, in hods.

*Pisthetaerus.* But how could they put the mortar into hods?

*Messenger.* Oh! 'twas a truly clever invention; the geese used their feet like spades; they buried them in the pile of mortar and then emptied them into the hods.

*Pisthetaerus.* Ah! to what use cannot feet be put?

*Messenger.* You should have seen how eagerly the ducks carried bricks. To complete the tale, the swallows came flying to the work, their beaks full of mortar and their trowel on their back, just the way little children are carried.

*Pisthetaerus.* Who would want paid servants after this? But, tell me, who did the woodwork?

*Messenger.* Birds again, and clever carpenters too, the pelicans, for they squared up the gates with their beaks in such a fashion that one would have thought they were using axes; the noise was just like a dockyard. Now the whole wall is tight everywhere, securely bolted and well guarded; it is patrolled, bell in hand; the sentinels stand everywhere and beacons burn on the towers. But I must run off to clean myself; the rest is your business.

*Chorus.* Well! what do you say to it? Are you not astonished at the wall being completed so quickly?

*Pisthetaerus.* By the gods, yes, and with good reason. 'Tis really not to be believed. But here comes another messenger from the wall to bring us some further news! What a fighting look he has!

*Second Messenger.* Oh! oh! oh! oh! oh! oh!

*Pisthetaerus.* What's the matter?

*Second Messenger.* A horrible outrage has occurred; a god sent by Zeus has passed through our gates and has penetrated the realms of the air without the knowledge of the jays, who are on guard in the daytime.

*Pisthetaerus.* 'Tis an unworthy and criminal deed. What god was it?

*Second Messenger.* We don't know that. All we know is, that he has got wings.

*Pisthetaerus.* Why were not guards sent against him at once?

*Second Messenger.* We have despatched thirty thousand hawks of the legion of mounted archers. All the hook-clawed birds are moving against him, the kestrel, the buzzard, the vulture, the great-horned owl; they cleave the air, so that it resounds with the flapping of their wings; they are looking everywhere for the god, who cannot be far away; indeed, if I mistake not, he is coming from yonder side.

*Pisthetaerus.* All arm themselves with slings and bows! This way, all our soldiers; shoot and strike! Some one give me a sling!

*Chorus.* War, a terrible war is breaking out between us and the gods! Come, let each one guard the Air, the son of Erebus, in which the clouds float. Take care no immortal enters it without your knowledge. Scan all sides with your glance. Hark! methinks I can hear the rustle of the swift wings of a god from heaven.

*Pisthetaerus.* Hi! you woman! where are you flying to? Halt, don't stir! keep motionless! not a beat of your wing! —Who are you and from what country? You must say whence you come.

*Iris.* I come from the abode of the Olympian gods.

*Pisthetaerus.* What's your name, ship or cap?

*Iris.* I am swift Iris.

*Pisthetaerus.* Paralus or Salaminia?

*Iris.* What do you mean?

*Pisthetaerus.* Let a buzzard rush at her and seize her.

*Iris.* Seize me! But what do all these insults betoken?

*Pisthetaerus.* Woe to you!

*Iris.* 'Tis incomprehensible.

*Pisthetaerus.* By which gate did you pass through the wall, wretched woman?

*Iris.* By which gate? Why, great gods, I don't know.

*Pisthetaerus.* You hear how she holds us in derision. Did you present yourself to the officers in command of the jays? You don't answer. Have you a permit, bearing the seal of the storks?

*Iris.* Am I awake?

*Pisthetaerus.* Did you get one?

*Iris.* Are you mad?

*Pisthetaerus.* No head-bird gave you a safe-conduct?

*Iris.* A safe-conduct to me, you poor fool!

*Pisthetaerus.* Ah! and so you slipped into this city on the sly and into these realms of air-land that don't belong to you.

*Iris.* And what other road can the gods travel?

*Pisthetaerus.* By Zeus! I know nothing about that, not I. But they won't pass this way. And you still dare to complain! Why, if you were treated according to your deserts, no Iris would ever have more justly suffered death.

*Iris.* I am immortal.

*Pisthetaerus.* You would have died nevertheless.—Oh! 'twould be truly intolerable! What! should the universe obey us and the gods alone continue their insolence and not understand that they must submit to the law of the strongest in their due turn? But tell me, where are you flying to?

*Iris.* I? The messenger of Zeus to mankind, I am going to tell them to sacrifice sheep and oxen on the altars and to fill their streets with the rich smoke of burning fat.

*Pisthetaerus.* Of which gods are you speaking?

*Iris.* Of which? Why, of ourselves, the gods of heaven.

*Pisthetaerus.* You, gods?

*Iris.* Are there others then?

*Pisthetaerus.* Men now adore the birds as gods, and 'tis to them, by Zeus, that they must offer sacrifices, and not to Zeus at all!

*Iris.* Oh! fool! fool! Rouse not the wrath of the gods, for 'tis terrible indeed. Armed with the brand of Zeus, Justice would annihilate your race; the lightning would strike you as it did Lycimnius and consume both your body and the porticos of your palace.

*Pisthetaerus.* Here! that's enough tall talk. Just you listen and keep quiet! Do you take me for a Lydian or a Phrygian and think to frighten me with your big words? Know, that if Zeus worries me again, I shall go at the head of my eagles, who are armed with lightning, and reduce his dwelling and that of Amphion to cinders. I shall send more than six hundred porphyrions clothed in leopards' skins up to heaven against him; and formerly a single Porphyrion gave him enough to do. As for you, his messenger, if you annoy me, I shall begin by stretching your legs asunder and so conduct myself, Iris though you be, that despite my age, you will be astonished. I will show you something that will make you three times over.

*Iris.* May you perish, you wretch, you and your infamous words!

*Pisthetaerus.* Won't you be off quickly? Come, stretch your wings or look out for squalls!

*Iris.* If my father does not punish you for your insults . . .

*Pisthetaerus.* Ha! . . . but just you be off elsewhere to roast younger folk than us with your lightning.

*Chorus.* We forbid the gods, the sons of Zeus, to pass through our city and the mortals to send them the smoke of their sacrifices by this road.

*Pisthetaerus.* 'Tis odd that the messenger we sent to the mortals has never returned.

*Herald.* Oh! blessed Pisthetaerus, very wise, very illustrious, very gracious, thrice happy, very . . . Come, prompt me, somebody, do.

*Pisthetaerus.* Get to your story!

*Herald.* All peoples are filled with admiration for your wisdom, and they award you this golden crown.

*Pisthetaerus.* I accept it. But tell me, why do the people admire me?

*Herald.* Oh you, who have founded so illustrious a city in the air, you know not in what esteem men hold you and how many there are who burn with desire to dwell in it. Before your city was built, all men had a mania for Sparta; long hair and fasting were held in honour, men went dirty like Socrates and carried staves. Now all is changed. Firstly, as soon as 'tis dawn, they all spring out of bed together to go and seek their food, the same as you do; then they fly off towards the notices and finally devour the decrees. The bird-madness is so clear, that many actually bear the names of birds. There is a halting victualler, who styles himself the partridge; Menippus calls himself the swallow; Opontius the one-eyed crow; Philocles the lark; Theogenes the fox-goose; Lycurgus the ibis; Chaerephon the bat; Syracosius the magpie; Midias the quail; indeed he looks like a quail that has been hit heavily over the head. Out of love for the birds they repeat all the songs which concern the swallow, the teal, the goose or the pigeon; in each verse you see wings, or at all events a few feathers. This is what is happening down there. Finally, there are more than ten thousand folk who are coming here from earth to ask you for feathers and hooked claws; so, mind you supply yourself with wings for the immigrants.

*Pisthetaerus.* Ah! by Zeus, 'tis not the time for idling. Go as quick as possible and fill every hamper, every basket you can find with wings. Manes will bring them to me outside the walls, where I will welcome those who present themselves.

*Chorus.* This town will soon be inhabited by a crowd of men.

*Pisthetaerus.* If fortune favours us.

*Chorus.* Folk are more and more delighted with it.

*Pisthetaerus.* Come, hurry up and bring them along.

*Chorus.* Will not man find here everything that can please him—wisdom, love, the divine Graces, the sweet face of gentle peace?

*Pisthetaerus.* Oh! you lazy servant! won't you hurry yourself?

*Chorus.* Let a basket of wings be brought speedily. Come, beat him as I do, and put some life into him; he is as lazy as an ass.

*Pisthetaerus.* Aye, Manes is a great craven.

*Chorus.* Begin by putting this heap of wings in order; divide them in three parts according to the birds from whom they came; the singing, the prophetic and the aquatic birds; then you must take care to distribute them to the men according to their character.

*Pisthetaerus (to Manes).* Oh! by the kestrels! I can keep my hands off you no longer; you are too slow and lazy altogether.

*A Parricide.* Oh! might I but become an eagle, who soars in the skies! Oh! might I fly above the azure waves of the barren sea!

*Pisthetaerus.* Ha! 'twould seem the news was true; I hear someone coming who talks of wings.

*Parricide.* Nothing is more charming than to fly; I burn with desire to live under the same laws as the birds; I am bird-mad and fly towards you, for I want to live with you and to obey your laws.

*Pisthetaerus.* Which laws? The birds have many laws.

*Parricide.* All of them; but the one that pleases me most is, that among the birds it is considered a fine thing to peck and strangle one's father.

*Pisthetaerus.* Aye, by Zeus! according to us, he who dares to strike his father, while still a chick, is a brave fellow.

*Parricide.* And therefore I want to dwell here, for I want to strangle my father and inherit his wealth.

*Pisthetaerus.* But we have also an ancient law written in the code of the storks, which runs thus, "When the stork father has reared his young and has taught them to fly, the young must in their turn support the father."

*Parricide.* 'Tis hardly worth while coming all this distance to be compelled to keep my father!

*Pisthetaerus.* No, no, young friend, since you have come to us with such willingness, I am going to give you these black wings, as though you were an orphan bird; furthermore, some good advice, that I received myself in infancy. Don't strike your father, but take these wings in one hand and these spurs in the other; imagine you have a cock's crest on your head and go and mount guard and fight; live on your pay and respect your father's life. You're a gallant fellow! Very well, then! Fly to Thrace and fight.

*Parricide.* By Bacchus! 'Tis well spoken; I will follow your counsel.

*Pisthetaerus.* 'Tis acting wisely, by Zeus.

*Cinesias.* "On my light pinions I soar off to Olympus; in its capricious flight my Muse flutters along the thousand paths of poetry in turn . . ."

*Pisthetaerus.* This is a fellow will need a whole shipload of wings.

*Cinesias.* ". . . and being fearless and vigorous, it is seeking fresh outlet."

*Pisthetaerus.* Welcome, Cinesias, you lime-wood man! Why have you come here a-twisting your game leg in circles?

*Cinesias.* "I want to become a bird, a tuneful nightingale."

*Pisthetaerus.* Enough of that sort of ditty. Tell me what you want.

*Cinesias.* Give me wings and I will fly into the topmost

airs to gather fresh songs in the clouds, in the midst of the vapours and the fleecy snow.

*Pisthetaerus.* Gather songs in the clouds?

*Cinesias.* 'Tis on them the whole of our latter-day art depends. The most brilliant dithyrambs are those that flap their wings in void space and are clothed in mist and dense obscurity. To appreciate this, just listen.

*Pisthetaerus.* Oh! no, no, no!

*Cinesias.* By Hermes! but indeed you shall. "I shall travel through thine ethereal empire like a winged bird, who cleaveth space with his long neck . . ."

*Pisthetaerus.* Stop! easy all, I say!

*Cinesias.* ". . . as I soar over the seas, carried by the breath of the winds . . ."

*Pisthetaerus.* By Zeus! but I'll cut your breath short.

*Cinesias.* ". . . now rushing along the tracks of Notus, now nearing Boreas across the infinite wastes of the ether." (*Pisthetaerus beats him.*) Ah! old man, that's a pretty and clever idea truly!

*Pisthetaerus.* What! are you not delighted to be cleaving the air?

*Cinesias.* To treat a dithyrambic poet, for whom the tribes dispute with each other, in this style!

*Pisthetaerus.* Will you stay with us and form a chorus of winged birds as slender as Leotrophides for the Cecropid tribe?

*Cinesias.* You are making game of me, 'tis clear; but know that I shall never leave you in peace if I do not have wings wherewith to traverse the air.

*An Informer.* What are these birds with downy feathers, who look so pitiable to me? Tell me, oh swallow with the long dappled wings.

*Pisthetaerus.* Oh! but 'tis a perfect invasion that threatens us. Here comes another of them, humming along.

*Informer.* Swallow with the long dappled wings, once more I summon you.

*Pisthetaerus.* It's his cloak I believe he's addressing; 'faith, it stands in great need of the swallows' return.

*Informer.* Where is he who gives our wings to all comers?

*Pisthetaerus.* 'Tis I, but you must tell me for what purpose you want them.

*Informer.* Ask no questions. I want wings, and wings I must have.

*Pisthetaerus.* Do you want to fly straight to Pellené?

*Informer.* I? Why, I am an accuser of the islands, an informer . . .

*Pisthetaerus.* A fine trade, truly!

*Informer.* . . . a hatcher of lawsuits. Hence I have great need of wings to prowl round the cities and drag them before justice.

*Pisthetaerus.* Would you do this better if you had wings?

*Informer.* No, but I should no longer fear the pirates; I should return with the cranes, loaded with a supply of lawsuits by way of ballast.

*Pisthetaerus.* So it seems, despite all your youthful vigour, you make it your trade to denounce strangers?

*Informer.* Well, and why not? I don't know how to dig.

*Pisthetaerus.* But, by Zeus! there are honest ways of gaining a living at your age without all this infamous trickery.

*Informer.* My friend, I am asking you for wings, not for words.

*Pisthetaerus.* 'Tis just my words that give you wings.

*Informer.* And how can you give a man wings with your words?

*Pisthetaerus.* 'Tis thus that all first start.

*Informer.* All?

*Pisthetaerus.* Have you not often heard the father say to young men in the barbers' shops, "It's astonishing how Diitrephes' advice has made my son fly to horse-riding."

—"Mine," says another, "has flown towards tragic poetry on the wings of his imagination."

*Informer.* So that words give wings?

*Pisthetaerus.* Undoubtedly; words give wings to the mind and make a man soar to heaven. Thus I hope that my wise words will give you wings to fly to some less degrading trade.

*Informer.* But I do not want to.

*Pisthetaerus.* What do you reckon on doing then?

*Informer.* I won't belie my breeding; from generation to generation we have lived by informing. Quick, therefore, give me quickly some light, swift hawk or kestrel wings, so that I may summon the islanders, sustain the accusation here, and haste back there again on flying pinions.

*Pisthetaerus.* I see. In this way the stranger will be condemned even before he appears.

*Informer.* That's just it.

*Pisthetaerus.* And while he is on his way here by sea, you will be flying to the islands to despoil him of his property.

*Informer.* You've hit it, precisely; I must whirl hither and thither like a perfect humming-top.

*Pisthetaerus.* I catch the idea. Wait, i' faith, I've got some fine Corcyraean wings. How do you like them?

*Informer.* Oh! woe is me! Why, 'tis a whip!

*Pisthetaerus.* No, no; these are the wings, I tell you, that set the top a-spinning.

*Informer.* Oh! oh! oh!

*Pisthetaerus.* Take your flight, clear off, you miserable cur, or you will soon see what comes of quibbling and lying. Come, let us gather up our wings and withdraw.

*Chorus.* In my ethereal flights I have seen many things new and strange and wondrous beyond belief. There is a tree called Cleonymus belonging to an unknown species; it has no heart, is good for nothing and is as tall as it is cowardly. In springtime it shoots forth calumnies instead of buds and in autumn it strews the ground with bucklers in place of leaves.

Far away in the regions of darkness, where no ray of light ever enters, there is a country, where men sit at the table of the heroes and dwell with them always—save always in the evening. Should any mortal meet the hero Orestes at night, he would soon be stripped and covered with blows from head to foot.

*Prometheus.* Ah! by the gods! if only Zeus does not espy me! Where is Pisthetaerus?

*Pisthetaerus.* Ha! what is this? A masked man!

*Prometheus.* Can you see any god behind me?

*Pisthetaerus.* No, none. But who are you, pray?

*Prometheus.* What's the time, please?

*Pisthetaerus.* The time? Why, it's past noon. Who are you?

*Prometheus.* Is it the fall of day? Is it no later than that?

*Pisthetaerus.* Oh! 'pon my word! but you grow tiresome!

*Prometheus.* What is Zeus doing? Is he dispersing the clouds or gathering them?

*Pisthetaerus.* Take care, lest I lose all patience.

*Prometheus.* Come, I will raise my mask.

*Pisthetaerus.* Ah! my dear Prometheus!

*Prometheus.* Stop! stop! speak lower!

*Pisthetaerus.* Why, what's the matter, Prometheus?

*Prometheus.* H'sh, h'sh! Don't call me by my name; you will be my ruin, if Zeus should see me here. But, if you want me to tell you how things are going in heaven, take this umbrella and shield me, so that the gods don't see me.

*Pisthetaerus.* I can recognize Prometheus in this cunning trick. Come, quick then, and fear nothing; speak on.

*Prometheus.* Then listen.

*Pisthetaerus.* I am listening, proceed!

*Prometheus.* It's all over with Zeus.

*Pisthetaerus.* Ah! and since when, pray?

*Prometheus.* Since you founded this city in the air. There is not a man who now sacrifices to the gods; the smoke of the victims no longer reaches us. Not the smallest offering comes! We fast as though it were the festival of Demeter. The barbarian gods, who are dying of hunger, are bawling like Illyrians and threaten to make an armed descent upon Zeus, if he does not open markets where joints of the victims are sold.

*Pisthetaerus.* What! there are other gods besides you, barbarian gods who dwell above Olympus?

*Prometheus.* If there were no barbarian gods, who would be the patron of Execestides?

*Pisthetaerus.* And what is the name of these gods?

*Prometheus.* Their name? Why, the Triballi.

*Pisthetaerus.* Ah, indeed! 'tis from that no doubt that we derive the word "tribulation."

*Prometheus.* Most likely. But one thing I can tell you for certain, namely, that Zeus and the celestial Triballi are going to send deputies here to sue for peace. Now don't you treat, unless Zeus restores the sceptre to the birds and gives you Basileia in marriage.

*Pisthetaerus.* Who is this Basileia?

*Prometheus.* A very fine young damsel, who makes the lightning for Zeus; all things come from her, wisdom, good laws, virtue, the fleet, calumnies, the public paymaster and the triobolus.

*Pisthetaerus.* Ah! then she is a sort of general manageress to the god.

*Prometheus.* Yes, precisely. If he gives you her for your wife, yours will be the almighty power. That is what I have come to tell you; for you know my constant and habitual goodwill towards men.

*Pisthetaerus.* Oh, yes! 'tis thanks to you that we roast our meat.

*Prometheus.* I hate the gods, as you know.

*Pisthetaerus.* Aye, by Zeus, you have always detested them.

*Prometheus.* Towards them I am a veritable Timon; but I must return in all haste, so give me the umbrella; if Zeus should see me from up there, he would think I was escorting one of the Canephori.

*Pisthetaerus.* Wait, take this stool as well.

*Chorus.* Near by the land of the Sciapodes there is a marsh, from the borders whereof the odious Socrates evokes the souls of men. Pisander came one day to see his soul, which he had left there when still alive. He offered a little victim, a camel, slit his throat and, following the example of Ulysses, stepped one pace backwards. Then that bat of a Chaerephon came up from hell to drink the camel's blood.

*Posidon.* This is the city of Nephelococcygia, Cloud-cuckoo-town, whither we come as ambassadors. (*To Triballus.*) Hi! what are you up to? you are throwing your cloak over the left shoulder. Come, fling it quick over the right! And why, pray, does it draggle in this fashion? Have you ulcers to hide like Laespodias? Oh! democracy! whither, oh! whither are you leading us? Is it possible that the gods have chosen such an envoy?

*Triballus.* Leave me alone.

*Posidon.* Ugh! the cursed savage! you are by far the most barbarous of all the gods.—Tell me, Heracles, what are we going to do?

*Heracles.* I have already told you that I want to strangle the fellow who has dared to block us in.

*Posidon.* But, my friend, we are envoys of peace.

*Heracles.* All the more reason why I wish to strangle him.

*Pisthetaerus.* Hand me the cheese-grater; bring me the silphium for sauce; pass me the cheese and watch the coals.

*Heracles.* Mortal! we who greet you are three gods.

*Pisthetaerus.* Wait a bit till I have prepared my silphium pickle.

*Heracles.* What are these meats?

*Pisthetaerus.* These are birds that have been punished with death for attacking the people's friends.

*Heracles.* And are you seasoning them before answering us?

*Pisthetaerus.* Ah! Heracles! welcome, welcome! What's the matter?

*Heracles.* The gods have sent us here as ambassadors to treat for peace.

*A Servant.* There's no more oil in the flask.

*Pisthetaerus.* And yet the birds must be thoroughly basted with it.

*Heracles.* We have no interest to serve in fighting you; as for you, be friends and we promise that you shall always have rain-water in your pools and the warmest of warm weather. So far as these points go we are armed with plenary authority.

*Pisthetaerus.* We have never been the aggressors, and even now we are as well disposed for peace as yourselves, provided you agree to one equitable condition, namely, that Zeus yield his sceptre to the birds. If only this is agreed to, I invite the ambassadors to dinner.

*Heracles.* That's good enough for me. I vote for peace.

*Posidon.* You wretch! you are nothing but a fool and a glutton. Do you want to dethrone your own father?

*Pisthetaerus.* What an error! Why, the gods will be much more powerful if the birds govern the earth. At present the mortals are hidden beneath the clouds, escape your observation, and commit perjury in your name; but if you had the birds for your allies, and a man, after having sworn by the crow and Zeus, should fail to keep his oath, the crow would dive down upon him unawares and pluck out his eye.

*Posidon.* Well thought of, by Posidon!

*Heracles.* My notion too.

*Pisthetaerus (to the Triballian).* And you, what's your opinion?

*Triballus.* Nabaisatreu.

*Pisthetaerus.* D'you see? he also approves. But hear another thing in which we can serve you. If a man vows to offer a sacrifice to some god, and then procrastinates, pretending that the gods can wait, and thus does not keep his word, we shall punish his stinginess.

*Posidon.* Ah! ah! and how?

*Pisthetaerus.* While he is counting his money or is in the bath, a kite will relieve him, before he knows it, either in coin or in clothes, of the value of a couple of sheep, and carry it to the god.

*Heracles.* I vote for restoring them the sceptre.

*Posidon.* Ask the Triballian.

*Heracles.* Hi! Triballian, do you want a thrashing?

*Triballus.* Saunaka baktarikrousa.

*Heracles.* He says, "Right willingly."

*Posidon.* If that be the opinion of both of you, why, I consent too.

*Heracles.* Very well! we accord the sceptre.

*Pisthetaerus.* Ah! I was nearly forgetting another condition. I will leave Heré to Zeus, but only if the young Basileia is given me in marriage.

*Posidon.* Then you don't want peace. Let us withdraw.

*Pisthetaerus.* It matters mighty little to me. Cook, look to the gravy.

*Heracles.* What an odd fellow this Posidon is! Where are you off to? Are we going to war about a woman?

*Posidon.* What else is there to do?

*Heracles.* What else? Why, conclude peace.

*Posidon.* Oh! the ninny! do you always want to be fooled? Why, you are seeking your own downfall. If Zeus were to die, after having yielded them the sovereignty, you would be ruined, for you are the heir of all the wealth he will leave behind.

*Pisthetaerus.* Oh! by the gods! how he is cajoling you. Step aside, that I may have a word with you. Your uncle is getting the better of you, my poor friend. The law will not allow you an obolus of the paternal property, for you are a bastard and not a legitimate child.

*Heracles.* I a bastard! What's that you tell me?

*Pisthetaerus.* Why, certainly; are you not born of a stranger woman? Besides, is not Athené recognized as Zeus' sole heiress? And no daughter would be that, if she had a legitimate brother.

*Heracles.* But what if my father wished to give me his property on his death-bed, even though I be a bastard?

*Pisthetaerus.* The law forbids it, and this same Posidon would be the first to lay claim to his wealth, in virtue of being his legitimate brother. Listen; thus runs Solon's law: "A bastard shall not inherit, if there are legitimate children; and if there are no legitimate children, the property shall pass to the nearest kin."

*Heracles.* And I get nothing whatever of the paternal property?

*Pisthetaerus.* Absolutely nothing. But tell me, has your father had you entered on the registers of his phratria?

*Heracles.* No, and I have long been surprised at the omission.

*Pisthetaerus.* What ails you, that you should shake your fist at heaven? Do you want to fight it? Why, be on my side, I will make you a king and will feed you on bird's milk and honey.

*Heracles.* Your further condition seems fair to me. I cede you the young damsel.

*Posidon.* But I, I vote against this opinion.

*Pisthetaerus.* Then all depends on the Triballian. (*To the Triballian.*) What do you say?

*Triballus.* Big bird give daughter pretty and queen.

*Heracles.* You say that you give her?

*Posidon.* Why no, he does not say anything of the sort, that he gives her; else I cannot understand any better than the swallows.

*Pisthetaerus.* Exactly so. Does he not say she must be given to the swallows?

*Posidon.* Very well! you two arrange the matter; make peace, since you wish it so; I'll hold my tongue.

*Heracles.* We are of a mind to grant you all that you ask. But come up there with us to receive Basileia and the celestial bounty.

*Pisthetaerus.* Here are birds already cut up, and very suitable for a nuptial feast.

*Heracles.* You go and, if you like, I will stay here to roast them.

*Pisthetaerus.* You to roast them! you are too much the glutton; come along with us.

*Heracles.* Ah! how well I would have treated myself!

*Pisthetaerus.* Let some bring me a beautiful and magnificent tunic for the wedding.

*Chorus.* At Phanae, near the Clepsydra, there dwells a people who have neither faith nor law, the Englottogastors, who reap, sow, pluck the vines and the figs with their tongues; they belong to a barbaric race, and among them the Philippi and the Gorgiases are to be found; 'tis these Englottogastorian Philippi who introduced the custom all over Attica of cutting out the tongue separately at sacrifices.

*A Messenger.* Oh, you, whose unbounded happiness I cannot express in words, thrice happy race of airy birds, receive your king in your fortunate dwellings. More brilliant than the brightest star that illumes the earth, he is approaching his glittering golden palace; the sun itself does not shine with more dazzling glory. He is entering with his bride at his side, whose beauty no human tongue can express; in his hand he brandishes the lightning, the winged shaft of Zeus; perfumes of unspeakable sweetness pervade the ethereal realms. 'Tis a glorious spectacle to see the clouds of incense wafting in light whirlwinds before the breath of the Zephyr! But here he is himself. Divine Muse! let thy sacred lips begin with songs of happy omen.

*Chorus.* Fall back! to the right! to the left! advance! Fly around this happy mortal, whom Fortune loads with her blessings. Oh! oh! what grace! what beauty! Oh, marriage so auspicious for our city! All honour to this man! 'tis through him that the birds are called to such glorious destinies. Let your nuptial hymns, your nuptial songs, greet him and his Basileia! 'Twas in the midst of such festivities that the Fates formerly united Olympian Heré to the King who governs the gods from the summit of his inaccessible throne. Oh! Hymen! oh! Hymenaeus! Rosy Eros with the golden wings held the reins and guided the chariot; 'twas he, who presided over the union of Zeus and the fortunate Heré. Oh! Hymen! oh! Hymenaeus!

*Pisthetaerus.* I am delighted with your songs, I applaud your verses. Now celebrate the thunder that shakes the earth, the flaming lightning of Zeus and the terrible flashing thunderbolt.

*Chorus.* Oh, thou golden flash of the lightning! oh, ye divine shafts of flame, that Zeus has hitherto shot forth! Oh, ye rolling thunders, that bring down the rain! 'Tis by the order of *our* king that ye shall now stagger the earth! Oh, Hymen! 'tis through thee that he commands the universe and that he makes Basileia, whom he has robbed from Zeus, take her seat at his side. Oh! Hymen! oh! Hymenaeus!

*Pisthetaerus.* Let all the winged tribes of our fellow-citizens follow the bridal couple to the palace of Zeus and to the nuptial couch! Stretch forth your hands, my dear wife! Take hold of me by my wings and let us dance; I am going to lift you up and carry you through the air.

*Chorus.* Oh, joy! Io Paean! Tralala! victory is thine, oh, thou greatest of the gods!

# THE CLOUDS

# THE CLOUDS

## *Dramatis Personae*

STREPSIADES.
PHIDIPPIDES.
SERVANT OF STREPSIADES.
SOCRATES.
DISCIPLES OF SOCRATES.
JUST DISCOURSE.
UNJUST DISCOURSE.
PASIAS, a Money-lender.
PASIAS' WITNESS.
AMYNIAS, another Money-lender.
CHAEREPHON.
CHORUS OF CLOUDS.

SCENE: A sleeping-room in Strepsiades' house;
  then in front of Socrates' house.

# THE CLOUDS

*Strepsiades*. Great gods! will these nights never end? will daylight never come? I heard the cock crow long ago and my slaves are snoring still! Ah! 'twas not so formerly. Curses on the War! has it not done me ills enough? Now I may not even chastise my own slaves. Again there's this brave lad, who never wakes the whole long night, but, wrapped in his five coverlets, farts away to his heart's content. Come! let me nestle in well and snore too, if it be possible . . . oh! misery, 'tis vain to think of sleep with all these expenses, this stable, these debts, which are devouring me, thanks to this fine cavalier, who only knows how to look after his long locks, to show himself off in his chariot and to dream of horses! And I, I am nearly dead, when I see the moon bringing the third decade in her train and my liability falling due. . . . Slave! light the lamp and bring me my tablets. Who are all my creditors? Let me see and reckon up the interest. What is it I owe? . . . Twelve minae to Pasias. . . . What! twelve minae to Pasias? . . . Why did I borrow these? Ah! I know! 'Twas to buy that thoroughbred, which cost me so dear. How I should have prized the stone that had blinded him!

121

*Phidippides* (*in his sleep*). That's not fair, Philo! Drive your chariot straight, I say.

*Strepsiades.* 'Tis this that is destroying me. He raves about horses, even in his sleep.

*Phidippides* (*still sleeping*). How many times round the track is the race for the chariots of war?

*Strepsiades.* 'Tis your own father you are driving to death . . . to ruin. Come! what debt comes next, after that of Pasias? . . . Three minae to Amynias for a chariot and its two wheels.

*Phidippides* (*still asleep*). Give the horse a good roll in the dust and lead him home.

*Strepsiades.* Ah! wretched boy! 'tis my money that you are making roll. My creditors have distrained on my goods, and here are others again, who demand security for their interest.

*Phidippides* (*awaking*). What is the matter with you, father, that you groan and turn about the whole night through?

*Strepsiades.* I have a bum-bailiff in the bedclothes biting me.

*Phidippides.* For pity's sake, let me have a little sleep.

*Strepsiades.* Very well, sleep on! but remember that all these debts will fall back on your shoulders. Oh! curses on the go-between who made me marry your mother! I lived so happily in the country, a commonplace, everyday life, but a good and easy one—had not a trouble, not a care, was rich in bees, in sheep and in olives. Then forsooth I must marry the niece of Megacles, the son of Megacles; I belonged to the country, she was from the town; she was a haughty, extravagant woman, a true Coesyra. On the nuptial day, when I lay beside her, I was reeking of the dregs of the wine-cup, of cheese and of wool; she was redolent with essences, saffron, tender kisses, the love of spending, of good cheer and of wanton delights. I will not say she did nothing; no, she worked hard . . . to ruin me, and pretending all the while merely to be showing her the cloak she had woven for me, I said, "Wife, you go too fast about your work, your threads are too closely woven and you use far too much wool."

*A Slave.* There is no more oil in the lamp.

*Strepsiades.* Why then did you light such a guzzling lamp? Come here, I am going to beat you!

*Slave.* What for?

*Strepsiades.* Because you have put in too thick a wick. . . . Later, when we had this boy, what was to be his name? 'Twas the cause of much quarrelling with my loving wife. She insisted on having some reference to a horse in his name, that he should be called Xanthippus, Charippus or Callippides. I wanted to name him Phidonides after his grandfather. We disputed long, and finally agreed to style him Phidippides. . . . She used to fondle and coax him, saying, "Oh! what a joy it will be to me when you have grown up, to see you, like my father, Megacles, clothed in purple and standing up straight in your chariot driving your steeds toward the town." And I would say to him, "When, like your father, you will go, dressed in a skin, to fetch back your goats from Phellus." Alas! he never listened to me and his madness for horses has shattered my fortune. But by dint of thinking the livelong night, I have discovered a road to salvation, both miraculous and divine. If he will but follow it, I shall be out of my trouble! First, however, he must be awakened, but let it be done as gently as possible. How shall I manage it? Phidippides! my little Phidippides!

*Phidippides.* What is it, father!

*Strepsiades.* Kiss me and give me your hand.

*Phidippides.* There! What's it all about?

*Strepsiades.* Tell me! do you love me?

*Phidippides.* By Posidon, the equestrian Posidon! yes, I swear I do.

*Strepsiades.* Oh, do not, I pray you, invoke this god of horses; 'tis he who is the cause of all my cares. But if you really love me, and with your whole heart, my boy, believe me.

*Phidippides.* Believe you? about what?

*Strepsiades.* Alter your habits forthwith and go and learn what I tell you.

*Phidippides.* Say on, what are your orders?

*Strepsiades.* Will you obey me ever so little?

*Phidippides.* By Bacchus, I will obey you.

*Strepsiades.* Very well then! Look this way. Do you see that little door and that little house?

*Phidippides.* Yes, father. But what are you driving at?

*Strepsiades.* That is the school of wisdom. There, they prove that we are coals enclosed on all sides under a vast extinguisher, which is the sky. If well paid, these men also teach one how to gain law-suits, whether they be just or not.

*Phidippides.* What do they call themselves?

*Strepsiades.* I do not know exactly, but they are deep thinkers and most admirable people.

*Phidippides.* Bah! the wretches! I know them; you mean those quacks with livid faces, those barefoot fellows, such as that miserable Socrates and Chaerephon?

*Strepsiades.* Silence! say nothing foolish! If you desire your father not to die of hunger, join their company and let your horses go.

*Phidippides.* No, by Bacchus! even though you gave me the pheasants that Leogoras rears.

*Strepsiades.* Oh! my beloved son, I beseech you, go and follow their teachings.

*Phidippides.* And what is it I should learn?

*Strepsiades.* 'Twould seem they have two courses of reasoning, the true and the false, and that, thanks to the false, the worst law-suits can be gained. If then you learn this science, which is false, I shall not pay an obolus of all the debts I have contracted on your account.

*Phidippides.* No, I will not do it. I should no longer dare to look at our gallant horsemen, when I had so tarnished my fair hue of honour.

*Strepsiades.* Well then, by Demeter! I will no longer support you, neither you, nor your team, nor your saddle-horse. Go and hang yourself, I turn you out of house and home.

*Phidippides.* My uncle Megacles will not leave me without horses; I shall go to him and laugh at your anger.

*Strepsiades.* One rebuff shall not dishearten me. With the help of the gods I will enter this school and learn myself. But at my age, memory has gone and the mind is slow to grasp things. How can all these fine distinctions, these subtleties be learned? Bah! why should I dally thus instead of rapping at the door? Slave, slave! (*He knocks and calls.*)

*A Disciple.* A plague on you! Who are you?

*Strepsiades.* Strepsiades, the son of Phido, of the deme of Cicynna.

*Disciple.* 'Tis for sure only an ignorant and illiterate fellow who lets drive at the door with such kicks. You have brought on a miscarriage—of an idea!

*Strepsiades.* Pardon me, pray; for I live far away from here in the country. But tell me, what was the idea that miscarried?

*Disciple.* I may not tell it to any but a disciple.

*Strepsiades.* Then tell me without fear, for I have come to study among you.

*Disciple.* Very well then, but reflect, that these are mysteries. Lately, a flea bit Chaerephon on the brow and then from there sprang on to the head of Socrates. Socrates asked Chaerephon, "How many times the length of its legs does a flea jump?"

*Strepsiades.* And how ever did he set about measuring it?

*Disciple.* Oh! 'twas most ingenious! He melted some wax, seized the flea and dipped its two feet in the wax, which, when cooled, left them shod with true Persian buskins. These he slipped off and with them measured the distance.

*Strepsiades.* Ah! great Zeus! what a brain! what subtlety!

*Disciple.* I wonder what then would you say, if you knew another of Socrates' contrivances?

*Strepsiades.* What is it? Pray tell me.

*Disciple.* Chaerephon of the deme of Sphettia asked him whether he thought a gnat buzzed through its proboscis or through its rear.

*Strepsiades.* And what did he say about the gnat?

*Disciple.* He said that the gut of the gnat was narrow, and that, in passing through this tiny passage, the air is driven with force towards the breech; then after this slender channel, it encountered the rump, which was distended like a trumpet, and there it resounded sonorously.

*Strepsiades.* So the rear of a gnat is a trumpet. Oh! what a splendid discovery! Thrice happy Socrates! 'Twould not be difficult to succeed in a law-suit, knowing so much about the gut of a gnat!

*Disciple.* Not long ago a lizard caused him the loss of a sublime thought.

*Strepsiades.* In what way, an it please you?

*Disciple.* One night, when he was studying the course of the moon and its revolutions and was gazing openmouthed at the heavens, a lizard crapped upon him from the top of the roof.

*Strepsiades*. This lizard, that relieved itself over Socrates, tickles me.

*Disciple*. Yesternight we had nothing to eat.

*Strepsiades*. Well! What did he contrive, to secure you some supper?

*Disciple*. He spread over the table a light layer of cinders, bending an iron rod the while; then he took up a pair of compasses and at the same moment unhooked a piece of the victim which was hanging in the palaestra.

*Strepsiades*. And we still dare to admire Thales! Open, open this home of knowledge to me quickly! Haste, haste to show me Socrates; I long to become his disciple. But do, do open the door. (*The disciple admits Strepsiades.*) Ah! by Heracles! what country are those animals from?

*Disciple*. Why, what are you astonished at? What do you think they resemble?

*Strepsiades*. The captives of Pylos. But why do they look so fixedly on the ground?

*Disciple*. They are seeking for what is below the ground.

*Strepsiades*. Ah! 'tis onions they are seeking. Do not give yourselves so much trouble; I know where there are some, fine and large ones. But what are those fellows doing, who are bent all double?

*Disciple*. They are sounding the abysses of Tartarus.

*Strepsiades*. And what is their rump looking at in the heavens?

*Disciple*. It is studying astronomy on its own account. But come in; so that the master may not find us here.

*Strepsiades*. Not yet, not yet; let them not change their position. I want to tell them my own little matter.

*Disciple*. But they may not stay too long in the open air and away from school.

*Strepsiades*. In the name of all the gods, what is that? Tell me. (*Pointing to a celestial globe.*)

*Disciple.* That is astronomy.

*Strepsiades.* And that? (*Pointing to a map.*)

*Disciple.* Geometry.

*Strepsiades.* What is that used for?

*Disciple.* To measure the land.

*Strepsiades.* But that is apportioned by lot.

*Disciple.* No, no, I mean the entire earth.

*Strepsiades.* Ah! what a funny thing! How generally useful indeed is this invention!

*Disciple.* There is the whole surface of the earth. Look! Here is Athens.

*Strepsiades.* Athens! you are mistaken; I see no courts sitting.

*Disciple.* Nevertheless it is really and truly the Attic territory.

*Strepsiades.* And where are my neighbours of Cicynna?

*Disciple.* They live here. This is Euboea; you see this island, that is so long and narrow.

*Strepsiades.* I know. 'Tis we and Pericles, who have stretched it by dint of squeezing it. And where is Lacedaemon?

*Disciple.* Lacedaemon? Why, here it is, look.

*Strepsiades.* How near it is to us! Think it well over, it must be removed to a greater distance.

*Disciple.* But, by Zeus, that is not possible.

*Strepsiades.* Then, woe to you! And who is this man suspended up in a basket?

*Disciple.* 'Tis *he himself.*

*Strepsiades.* Who himself?

*Disciple.* Socrates.

*Strepsiades.* Socrates! Oh! I pray you, call him right loudly for me.

*Disciple.* Call him yourself; I have no time to waste.

*Strepsiades.* Socrates! my little Socrates!

*Socrates.* Mortal, what do you want with me?

*Strepsiades.* First, what are you doing up there? Tell me, I beseech you.

*Socrates.* I traverse the air and contemplate the sun.

*Strepsiades.* Thus 'tis not on the solid ground, but from the height of this basket, that you slight the gods, if indeed . . .

*Socrates.* I have to suspend my brain and mingle the subtle essence of my mind with this air, which is of the like nature, in order to clearly penetrate the things of heaven. I should have discovered nothing, had I remained on the ground to consider from below the things that are above; for the earth by its force attracts the sap of the mind to itself. 'Tis just the same with the water-cress.

*Strepsiades.* What? Does the mind attract the sap of the water-cress? Ah! my dear little Socrates, come down to me! I have come to ask you for lessons.

*Socrates.* And for what lessons?

*Strepsiades.* I want to learn how to speak. I have borrowed money, and my merciless creditors do not leave me a moment's peace; all my goods are at stake.

*Socrates.* And how was it you did not see that you were getting so much into debt?

*Strepsiades.* My ruin has been the madness of horses, a most rapacious evil; but teach me one of your two methods of reasoning, the one whose object is not to repay anything, and, may the gods bear witness, that I am ready to pay any fee you may name.

*Socrates.* By which gods will you swear? To begin with, the gods are not a coin current with us.

*Strepsiades.* But what do you swear by then? By the iron money of Byzantium?

*Socrates.* Do you really wish to know the truth of celestial matters?

*Strepsiades.* Why, truly, if 'tis possible.

*Socrates*. . . . and to converse with the clouds, who are our genii?

*Strepsiades*. Without a doubt.

*Socrates*. Then be seated on this sacred couch.

*Strepsiades*. I am seated.

*Socrates*. Now take this chaplet.

*Strepsiades*. Why a chaplet? Alas! Socrates, would you sacrifice me, like Athamas?

*Socrates*. No, these are the rites of initiation.

*Strepsiades*. And what is it I am to gain?

*Socrates*. You will become a thorough rattle-pate, a hardened old stager, the fine flour of the talkers. . . . But come, keep quiet.

*Strepsiades*. By Zeus! You lie not! Soon I shall be nothing but wheat-flour, if you powder me in this fashion.

*Socrates*. Silence, old man, give heed to the prayers. . . . Oh! most mighty king, the boundless air, that keepest the earth suspended in space, thou bright Aether and ye venerable goddesses, the Clouds, who carry in your loins the thunder and the lightning, arise, ye sovereign powers and manifest yourselves in the celestial spheres to the eyes of the sage.

*Strepsiades*. Not yet! Wait a bit, till I fold my mantle double, so as not to get wet. And to think that I did not even bring my travelling cap! What a misfortune!

*Socrates*. Come, oh! Clouds, whom I adore, come and show yourselves to this man, whether you be resting on the sacred summits of Olympus, crowned with hoar-frost, or tarrying in the gardens of Ocean, your father, forming sacred choruses with the Nymphs; whether you be gathering the waves of the Nile in golden vases or dwelling in the Maeotic marsh or on the snowy rocks of Mimas, hearken to my prayer and accept my offering. May these sacrifices be pleasing to you.

*Chorus.* Eternal Clouds, let us appear, let us arise from the roaring depths of Ocean, our father; let us fly towards the lofty mountains, spread our damp wings over their forest-laden summits, whence we will dominate the distant valleys, the harvest fed by the sacred earth, the murmur of the divine streams and the resounding waves of the sea, which the unwearying orb lights up with its glittering beams. But let us shake off the rainy fogs, which hide our immortal beauty and sweep the earth from afar with our gaze.

*Socrates.* Oh, venerated goddesses, yes, you are answering my call! (*To Strepsiades.*) Did you hear their voices mingling with the awful growling of the thunder?

*Strepsiades.* Oh! adorable Clouds, I revere you and I too am going to let off *my* thunder, so greatly has your own affrighted me. Faith! whether permitted or not, I must, I must crap!

*Socrates.* No scoffing; do not copy those accursed comic poets. Come, silence! a numerous host of goddesses approaches with songs.

*Chorus.* Virgins, who pour forth the rains, let us move toward Attica, the rich country of Pallas, the home of the brave; let us visit the dear land of Cecrops, where the secret rites are celebrated, where the mysterious sanctuary flies open to the initiate. . . . What victims are offered there to the deities of heaven! What glorious temples! What statues! What holy prayers to the rulers of Olympus! At every season nothing but sacred festivals, garlanded victims, are to be seen. Then Spring brings round again the joyous feasts of Dionysus, the harmonious contests of the choruses and the serious melodies of the flute.

*Strepsiades.* By Zeus! Tell me, Socrates, I pray you, who are these women, whose language is so solemn; can they be demi-goddesses?

*Socrates.* Not at all. They are the Clouds of heaven, great goddesses for the lazy; to them we owe all, thoughts, speeches, trickery, roguery, boasting, lies, sagacity.

*Strepsiades.* Ah! that was why, as I listened to them, my mind spread out its wings; it burns to babble about trifles, to maintain worthless arguments, to voice its petty reasons, to contradict, to tease some opponent. But are they not going to show themselves? I should like to see them, were it possible.

*Socrates.* Well, look this way in the direction of Parnes; I already see those who are slowly descending.

*Strepsiades.* But where, where? Show them to me.

*Socrates.* They are advancing in a throng, following an oblique path across the dales and thickets.

*Strepsiades.* 'Tis strange! I can see nothing.

*Socrates.* There, close to the entrance.

*Strepsiades.* Hardly, if at all, can I distinguish them.

*Socrates.* You *must* see them clearly now, unless your eyes are filled with gum as thick as pumpkins.

*Strepsiades.* Aye, undoubtedly! Oh! the venerable goddesses! Why, they fill up the entire stage.

*Socrates.* And you did not know, you never suspected, that they were goddesses?

*Strepsiades.* No, indeed; methought the Clouds were only fog, dew and vapour.

*Socrates.* But what you certainly do not know is that they are the support of a crowd of quacks, both the diviners, who were sent to Thurium, the notorious physicians, the well-combed fops, who load their fingers with rings down to the nails, and the braggarts, who write dithyrambic verses, all these are idlers whom the Clouds provide a living for, because they sing them in their verses.

*Strepsiades.* 'Tis then for this that they praise "the rapid flight of the moist clouds, which veil the brightness of day" and "the waving locks of the hundred-headed Typho" and "the impetuous tempests, which float through the heavens, like birds of prey with aerial wings, loaded with mists" and "the rains, the dew, which the clouds outpour." As a reward for these fine phrases they bolt wellgrown, tasty mullet and delicate thrushes.

*Socrates.* Yes, thanks to these. And is it not right and meet?

*Strepsiades.* Tell me then why, if these really are the Clouds, they so very much resemble mortals. This is not their usual form.

*Socrates.* What are they like then?

*Strepsiades.* I don't know exactly; well, they are like great packs of wool, but not like women—no, not in the least. . . . And these have noses.

*Socrates.* Answer my questions.

*Strepsiades.* Willingly! Go on, I am listening.

*Socrates.* Have you not sometimes seen clouds in the sky like a centaur, a leopard, a wolf or a bull?

*Strepsiades.* Why, certainly I have, but what then?

*Socrates.* They take what metamorphosis they like. If they see a debauchee with long flowing locks and hairy as a beast, like the son of Xenophantes, they take the form of a Centaur in derision of his shameful passion.

*Strepsiades.* And when they see Simon, that thiever of public money, what do they do then?

*Socrates.* To picture him to the life, they turn at once into wolves.

*Strepsiades.* So that was why yesterday, when they saw Cleonymus, who cast away his buckler because he is the veriest poltroon amongst men, they changed into deer.

*Socrates.* And to-day they have seen Clisthenes; you see . . . they are women.

*Strepsiades.* Hail, sovereign goddesses, and if ever you

have let your celestial voice be heard by mortal ears, speak to me, oh! speak to me, ye all-powerful queens.

*Chorus.* Hail! veteran of the ancient times, you who burn to instruct yourself in fine language. And you, great high-priest of subtle nonsense, tell us your desire. To you and Prodicus alone of all the hollow orationers of to-day have we lent an ear—to Prodicus, because of his knowledge and his great wisdom, and to you, because you walk with head erect, a confident look, barefooted, resigned to everything and proud of our protection.

*Strepsiades.* Oh! Earth! What august utterances! how sacred! how wondrous!

*Socrates.* That is because these are the only goddesses; all the rest are pure myth.

*Strepsiades.* But by the Earth! is our Father, Zeus, the Olympian, not a god?

*Socrates.* Zeus! what Zeus? Are you mad? There is no Zeus.

*Strepsiades.* What are you saying now? Who causes the rain to fall? Answer me that!

*Socrates.* Why, 'tis these, and I will prove it. Have you ever seen it raining without clouds? Let Zeus then cause rain with a clear sky and without their presence!

*Strepsiades.* By Apollo! that is powerfully argued! For my own part, I always thought it was Zeus pissing into a sieve. But tell me, who is it makes the thunder, which I so much dread?

*Socrates.* 'Tis these, when they roll one over the other.

*Strepsiades.* But how can that be? you most daring among men!

*Socrates.* Being full of water, and forced to move along, they are of necessity precipitated in rain, being fully distended with moisture from the regions where they have been floating; hence they bump each other heavily and burst with great noise.

*Strepsiades.* But is it not Zeus who forces them to move?

*Socrates.* Not at all; 'tis aerial Whirlwind.

*Strepsiades.* The Whirlwind! ah! I did not know that. So Zeus, it seems, has no existence, and 'tis the Whirlwind that reigns in his stead? But you have not yet told me what makes the roll of the thunder?

*Socrates.* Have you not understood me then? I tell you, that the Clouds, when full of rain, bump against one another, and that, being inordinately swollen out, they burst with a great noise.

*Strepsiades.* How can you make me credit that?

*Socrates.* Take yourself as an example. When you have heartily gorged on stew at the Panathenaea, you get throes of stomach-ache and then suddenly your belly resounds with prolonged growling.

*Strepsiades.* Yes, yes, by Apollo! I suffer, I get colic, then the stew sets a-growling like thunder and finally bursts forth with a terrific noise. At first, 'tis but a little gurgling *pappax, pappax!* then it increases, *papapap-pax!* and when I seek relief, why, 'tis thunder indeed, *papa-pappax! pappax!! papapapappax!!!* just like the clouds.

*Socrates.* Well then, reflect what a noise is produced by your belly, which is but small. Shall not the air, which is boundless, produce these mighty claps of thunder?

*Strepsiades.* But tell me this. Whence comes the lightning, the dazzling flame, which at times consumes the man it strikes, at others hardly singes him. Is it not plain, that 'tis Zeus hurling it at the perjurers?

*Socrates.* Out upon the fool! the driveller! he still savours of the golden age! If Zeus strikes at the perjurers, why has he not blasted Simon, Cleonymus and Theorus? Of a surety, greater perjurers cannot exist. No, he strikes his own Temple, and Sunium, the promontory of Athens, and the towering oaks. Now, why should he do that? An oak is no perjurer.

*Strepsiades.* I cannot tell, but it seems to me well argued. What is the thunder then?

*Socrates.* When a dry wind ascends to the Clouds and gets shut into them, it blows them out like a bladder; finally, being too confined, it bursts them, escapes with fierce violence and a roar to flash into flame by reason of its own impetuosity.

*Strepsiades.* Forsooth, 'tis just what happened to me one day. 'Twas at the feast of Zeus! I was cooking a sow's belly for my family and I had forgotten to slit it open. It swelled out and, suddenly bursting, discharged itself right into my eyes and burnt my face.

*Chorus.* Oh, mortal! you, who desire to instruct yourself in our great wisdom, the Athenians, the Greeks will envy you your good fortune. Only you must have the memory and ardour for study, you must know how to stand the tests, hold your own, go forward without feeling fatigue, caring but little for food, abstaining from wine, gymnastic exercises and other similar follies, in fact, you must believe as every man of intellect should, that the greatest of all blessings is to live and think more clearly than the vulgar herd, to shine in the contests of words.

*Strepsiades.* If it be a question of hardiness for labour, of spending whole nights at work, of living sparingly, of fighting my stomach and only eating chick-pease, rest assured, I am as hard as an anvil.

*Socrates.* Henceforward, following our example, you will recognize no other gods but Chaos, the Clouds and the Tongue, these three alone.

*Strepsiades.* I would not speak to the others, even if I should meet them in the street; not a single sacrifice, not a libation, not a grain of incense for them!

*Chorus.* Tell us boldly then what you want of us; you

cannot fail to succeed, if you honour and revere us and if you are resolved to become a clever man.

*Strepsiades.* Oh, sovereign goddesses, 'tis but a very small favor that I ask of you; grant that I may distance all the Greeks by a hundred stadia in the art of speaking.

*Chorus.* We grant you this, and henceforward no eloquence shall more often succeed with the people than your own.

*Strepsiades.* May the god shield me from possessing great eloquence! 'Tis not what I want. I want to be able to turn bad law-suits to my own advantage and to slip through the fingers of my creditors.

*Chorus.* It shall be as you wish, for your ambitions are modest. Commit yourself fearlessly to our ministers, the sophists.

*Strepsiades.* This will I do, for I trust in you. Moreover there is no drawing back, what with these cursed horses and this marriage, which has eaten up my vitals. So let them do with me as they will; I yield my body to them. Come blows, come hunger, thirst, heat or cold, little matters it to me; they may flay me, if I only escape my debts, if only I win the reputation of being a bold rascal, a fine speaker, impudent, shameless, a braggart, and adept at stringing lies, an old stager at quibbles, a complete table of the laws, a thorough rattle, a fox to slip through any hole; supple as a leathern strap, slippery as an eel, an artful fellow, a blusterer, a villain; a knave with a hundred faces, cunning, intolerable, a gluttonous dog. With such epithets do I seek to be greeted; on these terms they can treat me as they choose, and, if they wish, by Demeter! they can turn me into sausages and serve me up to the philosophers.

*Chorus.* Here have we a bold and well-disposed pupil indeed. When we shall have taught you, your glory among the mortals will reach even to the skies.

*Strepsiades.* Wherein will that profit me?

*Chorus.* You will pass your whole life among us and will be the most envied of men.

*Strepsiades.* Shall I really ever see such happiness?

*Chorus.* Clients will be everlastingly besieging your door in crowds, burning to get at you, to explain their business to you and to consult you about their suits, which, in return for your ability, will bring you in great sums. But, Socrates, begin the lessons you want to teach this old man; rouse his mind, try the strength of his intelligence.

*Socrates.* Come, tell me the kind of mind you have; 'tis important I know this, that I may order my batteries against you in a new fashion.

*Strepsiades.* Eh, what! in the name of the gods, are you purposing to assault me then?

*Socrates.* No. I only wish to ask you some questions. Have you any memory?

*Strepsiades.* That depends: if anything is owed me, my memory is excellent, but if I owe, alas! I have none whatever.

*Socrates.* Have you a natural gift for speaking?

*Strepsiades.* For speaking, no; for cheating, yes.

*Socrates.* How will you be able to learn then?

*Strepsiades.* Very easily, have no fear.

*Socrates.* Thus, when I throw forth some philosophical thought anent things celestial, you will seize it in its very flight?

*Strepsiades.* Then I am to snap up wisdom much as a dog snaps up a morsel?

*Socrates.* Oh! the ignoramus! the barbarian! I greatly fear, old man, 'twill be needful for me to have recourse to blows. Now, let me hear what you do when you are beaten.

*Strepsiades.* I receive the blow, then wait a moment,

take my witnesses and finally summon my assailant at
law.

*Socrates.* Come, take off your cloak.

*Strepsiades.* Have I robbed you of anything?

*Socrates.* No, but 'tis usual to enter the school without
your cloak.

*Strepsiades.* But I am not come here to look for stolen
goods.

*Socrates.* Off with it, fool!

*Strepsiades.* Tell me, if I prove thoroughly attentive
and learn with zeal, which of your disciples shall I resemble, do you think?

*Socrates.* You will be the image of Chaerephon.

*Strepsiades.* Ah! unhappy me! I shall then be but half
alive?

*Socrates.* A truce to this chatter! follow me and no
more of it.

*Strepsiades.* First give me a honey-cake, for to descend
down there sets me all a-tremble; meseems 'tis the cave of
Trophonius.

*Socrates.* But get in with you! What reason have you
for thus dallying at the door?

*Chorus.* Good luck! you have courage; may you succeed, you, who, though already so advanced in years,
wish to instruct your mind with new studies and practise
it in wisdom!

*Chorus* (*Parabasis*). Spectators! By Bacchus, whose
servant I am, I will frankly tell you the truth. May I secure both victory and renown as certainly as I hold you
for adept critics and as I regard this comedy as my best.
I wished to give you the first view of a work, which had
cost me much trouble, but I withdrew, unjustly beaten by
unskilful rivals. 'Tis you, oh, enlightened public, for
whom I have prepared my piece, that I reproach with
this. Nevertheless I shall never willingly cease to seek

the approval of the discerning. I have not forgotten the day, when men, whom one is happy to have for an audience, received my 'Young Man' and my 'Debauchee' with so much favour in this very place. Then as yet virgin, my Muse had not attained the legal age for maternity; she had to expose her first-born for another to adopt, and it has since grown up under your generous patronage. Ever since you have as good as sworn me your faithful alliance. Thus, like Electra of the poets, my comedy has come to seek you to-day, hoping again to encounter such enlightened spectators. As far away as she can discern her Orestes, she will be able to recognize him by his curly head. And note her modest demeanour! She has not sewn on a piece of hanging leather, thick and reddened at the end, to cause laughter among the children; she does not rail at the bald, neither does she dance the cordax; no old man is seen, who, while uttering his lines, batters his questioner with a stick to make his poor jests pass muster. She does not rush upon the scene carrying a torch and screaming, 'La, la! la, la!' No, she relies upon herself and her verses. . . . My value is so well known, that I take no further pride in it. I do not seek to deceive you, by reproducing the same subjects two or three times; I always invent fresh themes to present before you, themes that have no relation to each other and that are all clever. I attacked Cleon to his face and when he was all-powerful; but he has fallen, and now I have no desire to kick him when he is down. My rivals, on the contrary, once that this wretched Hyperbolus has given them the cue, have never ceased setting upon both him and his mother. First Eupolis presented his 'Maricas'; this was simply my 'Knights,' whom this plagiarist had clumsily furbished up again by adding to the piece an old drunken woman, so that she might dance the cordax. 'Twas an old idea, taken from Phrynichus, who caused his old hag to be devoured by a monster of the deep. Then Hermippus fell foul of Hyperbolus and now all the others fall upon him and repeat my comparison of the eels. May those who find amusement in their pieces not be pleased with mine, but as for you, who love and applaud my inventions, why, posterity will praise your good taste.

Oh, ruler of Olympus, all-powerful king of the gods, great Zeus, it is thou whom I first invoke; protect this chorus; and thou too, Posidon, whose dread trident upheaves at the will of thy anger both the bowels of the earth and the salty waves of the ocean. I invoke my illustrious father, the divine Aether, the universal sustainer of life, and Phoebus, who, from the summit of his chariot, sets the world aflame with his dazzling rays, Phoebus, a mighty deity amongst the gods and adored amongst mortals.

Most wise spectators, lend us all your attention. Give heed to our just reproaches. There exist no gods to whom this city owes more than it does to us, whom alone you forget. Not a sacrifice, not a libation is there for those who protect you! Have you decreed some mad expedition? Well! we thunder or we fall down in rain. When you chose that enemy of heaven, the Paphlagonian tanner, for a general, we knitted our brow, we caused our wrath to break out; the lightning shot forth, the thunder pealed, the moon deserted her course and the sun at once veiled his beam threatening no longer to give you light, if Cleon became general. Nevertheless you elected him; 'tis said, Athens never resolves upon some fatal step but the gods turn these errors into her greatest gain. Do you wish that this election should even now be a success for you? 'Tis a very simple thing to do; condemn this rapacious gull named Cleon for bribery and extortion, fit a wooden collar tight round his neck, and your error will be rectified and the commonweal will at once regain its old prosperity.

Aid me also, Phoebus, god of Delos, who reignest on the cragged peaks of Cynthia; and thou, happy virgin, to whom the Lydian damsels offer pompous sacrifice in a temple of gold; and thou, goddess of our country, Athené, armed with the aegis, the protectress of Athens; and thou, who, surrounded by the Bacchanals of Delphi, roamest over the rocks of Parnassus shaking the flame of thy resinous torch, thou, Bacchus, the god of revel and joy.

As we were preparing to come here, we were hailed by the Moon and were charged to wish joy and happiness both to the Athenians and to their allies; further, she said that she was enraged and that you treated her very shamefully, her, who does not pay you in words alone, but who renders you all real benefits. Firstly, thanks to her, you save at least a drachma each month for lights, for each, as he is leaving home at night, says, "Slave, buy no torches, for the moonlight is beautiful,"—not to name a thousand other benefits. Nevertheless you do not reckon the days correctly and your calendar is naught but confusion. Consequently the gods load her with threats each time they get home and are disappointed of their meal, because the festival has not been kept in the regular order of time. When you should be sacrificing, you are putting to the torture or administering justice. And often, we others, the gods, are fasting in token of mourning for the death of Memnon or Sarpedon, while you are devoting yourselves to joyous libations. 'Tis for this, that last year, when the lot would have invested Hyperbolus with the duty of Amphictyon, we took his crown from him, to teach him that time must be divided according to the phases of the moon.

*Socrates.* By Respiration, the Breath of Life! By Chaos!

By the Air! I have never seen a man so gross, so inept, so stupid, so forgetful. All the little quibbles, which I teach him, he forgets even before he has learnt them. Yet I will not give it up, I will make him come out here into the open air. Where are you, Strepsiades? Come, bring your couch out here.

*Strepsiades.* But the bugs will not allow me to bring it.

*Socrates.* Have done with such nonsense! place it there and pay attention.

*Strepsiades.* Well, here I am.

*Socrates.* Good! Which science of all those you have never been taught, do you wish to learn first? The measures, the rhythms or the verses?

*Strepsiades.* Why, the measures; the flour dealer cheated me out of two *choenixes* the other day.

*Socrates.* 'Tis not about that I ask you, but which, according to you, is the best measure, the trimeter or the tetrameter?

*Strepsiades.* The one I prefer is the semisextarius.

*Socrates.* You talk nonsense, my good fellow.

*Strepsiades.* I will wager your tetrameter is the semisextarius.

*Socrates.* Plague seize the dunce and the fool! Come, perchance you will learn the rhythms quicker.

*Strepsiades.* Will the rhythms supply me with food?

*Socrates.* First they will help you to be pleasant in company, then to know what is meant by oenoplian rhythm and what by the dactylic.

*Strepsiades.* Of the dactyl? I know that quite well.

*Socrates.* What is it then?

*Strepsiades.* Why, 'tis this finger; formerly, when a child, I used this one.

*Socrates.* You are as low-minded as you are stupid.

*Strepsiades.* But, wretched man, I do not want to learn all this.

*Socrates.* Then what *do* you want to know?

*Strepsiades.* Not that, not that, but the art of false reasoning.

*Socrates.* But you must first learn other things. Come, what are the male quadrupeds?

*Strepsiades.* Oh! I know the males thoroughly. Do not take me for a fool then! The ram, the buck, the bull, the dog, the pigeon.

*Socrates.* Do you see what you are doing; is not the female pigeon called the same as the male?

*Strepsiades.* How else? Come now.

*Socrates.* How else? With you then 'tis pigeon and pigeon!

*Strepsiades.* 'Tis true, by Posidon! but what names do you want me to give them?

*Socrates.* Term the female pigeonnette and the male pigeon.

*Strepsiades.* Pigeonnette! hah! by the Air! That's splendid! for that lesson bring out your kneading-trough and I will fill him with flour to the brim.

*Socrates.* There you are wrong again; you make *trough* masculine and it should be feminine.

*Strepsiades.* What? if say *him*, do I make the *trough* masculine?

*Socrates.* Assuredly! would you not say him for Cleonymus?

*Strepsiades.* Well?

*Socrates.* Then trough is of the same gender as Cleonymus?

*Strepsiades.* Oh! good sir! Cleonymus never had a kneading-trough; he used a round mortar for the purpose. But come, tell me what I *should* say?

*Socrates.* For trough you should say her as you would for Sostraté.

*Strepsiades.* Her?

*Socrates.* In this manner you make it truly female.

*Strepsiades.* That's it! *Her* for trough and *her* for Cleonymus.

*Socrates.* Now I must teach you to distinguish the masculine proper names from those that are feminine.

*Strepsiades.* Ah! I know the female names well.

*Socrates.* Name some then.

*Strepsiades.* Lysilla, Philinna, Clitagora, Demetria.

*Socrates.* And what are masculine names?

*Strepsiades.* They are countless—Philoxenus, Melesias, Amynias.

*Socrates.* But, wretched man, the last two are not masculine.

*Strepsiades.* You do not reckon them masculine?

*Socrates.* Not at all. If you met Amynias, how would you hail him?

*Strepsiades.* How? Why, I should shout, "Hi, hither, Amynia!"

*Socrates.* Do you see? 'tis a female name that you give him.

*Strepsiades.* And is it not rightly done, since he refuses military service? But what use is there in learning what we all know?

*Socrates.* You know nothing about it. Come, lie down there.

*Strepsiades.* What for?

*Socrates.* Ponder a while over matters that interest you.

*Strepsiades.* Oh! I pray you, not there! but, if I must lie down and ponder, let me lie on the ground.

*Socrates.* 'Tis out of the question. Come! on to the couch!

*Strepsiades.* What cruel fate! What a torture the bugs will this day put me to!

*Socrates.* Ponder and examine closely, gather your thoughts together, let your mind turn to every side of things; if you meet with a difficulty, spring quickly to some other idea; above all, keep your eyes away from all gentle sleep.

*Strepsiades.* Oh, woe, woe! oh, woe, woe!

*Socrates.* What ails you? why do you cry so?

*Strepsiades.* Oh! I am a dead man! Here are these cursed Corinthians advancing upon me from all corners of the couch; they are biting me, they are gnawing at my sides, they are drinking all my blood, they are twitching off my testicles, they are exploring all up my back, they are killing me!

*Socrates.* Not so much wailing and clamour, if you please.

*Strepsiades.* How can I obey? I have lost my money and my complexion, my blood and my slippers, and to cap my misery, I must keep awake on this couch, when scarce a breath of life is left in me.

*Socrates.* Well now! what are you doing? are you reflecting?

*Strepsiades.* Yes, by Posidon!

*Socrates.* What about?

*Strepsiades.* Whether the bugs will not entirely devour me.

*Socrates.* May death seize you, accursed man!

*Strepsiades.* Ah! it has already.

*Socrates.* Come, no giving way! Cover up your head; the thing to do is to find an ingenious alternative.

*Strepsiades.* An alternative! ah! I only wish one would come to me from within these coverlets!

*Socrates.* Hold! let us see what our fellow is doing! Ho! you! are you asleep?

*Strepsiades.* No, by Apollo!

*Socrates.* Have you got hold of anything?

*Strepsiades.* No, nothing whatever.

*Socrates.* Nothing at all!

*Strepsiades.* No, nothing except this, which I've got in my hand.

*Socrates.* Are you not going to cover your head immediately and ponder?

*Strepsiades.* Over what? Come, Socrates, tell me.

*Socrates.* Think first what you want, and then tell me.

*Strepsiades.* But I have told you a thousand times what I want. 'Tis not to pay any of my creditors.

*Socrates.* Come, wrap yourself up; consecrate your mind, which wanders too lightly, study every detail, scheme and examine thoroughly.

*Strepsiades.* Oh, woe! woe! oh dear! oh dear!

*Socrates.* Keep yourself quiet, and if any notion troubles you, put it quickly aside, then resume it and think over it again.

*Strepsiades.* My dear little Socrates!

*Socrates.* What is it; old greybeard?

*Strepsiades.* I have a scheme for not paying my debts.

*Socrates.* Let us hear it.

*Strepsiades.* Tell me, if I purchased a Thessalian witch, I could make the moon descend during the night and shut it, like a mirror, into a round box and there keep it carefully. . . .

*Socrates.* How would you gain by that?

*Strepsiades.* How? why, if the moon did not rise, I would have no interest to pay.

*Socrates.* Why so?

*Strepsiades.* Because money is lent by the month.

*Socrates.* Good! but I am going to propose another trick to you. If you were condemned to pay five talents, how would you manage to quash that verdict? Tell me.

*Strepsiades.* How? how? I don't know, I must think.

*Socrates.* Do you always shut your thoughts within yourself? Let your ideas fly in the air, like a may-bug, tied by the foot with a thread.

*Strepsiades.* I have found a very clever way to annul that conviction; you will admit that much yourself.

*Socrates.* What is it?

*Strepsiades.* Have you even seen a beautiful, transparent stone at the druggists, with which you may kindle fire?

*Socrates.* You mean a crystal lens.

*Strepsiades.* Yes.

*Socrates.* Well, what then?

*Strepsiades.* If I placed myself with this stone in the sun and a long way off from the clerk, while he was writing out the conviction, I could make all the wax, upon which the words were written, melt.

*Socrates.* Well thought out, by the Graces!

*Strepsiades.* Ah, I am delighted to have annulled the decree that was to cost me five talents.

*Socrates.* Come, take up this next question quickly.

*Strepsiades.* Which?

*Socrates.* If, when summoned to court, you were in danger of losing your case for want of witnesses, how would you make the conviction fall upon your opponent?

*Strepsiades.* 'Tis very simple and most easy.

*Socrates.* Let me hear.

*Strepsiades.* This way. If another case had to be pleaded before mine was called, I should run and hang myself.

*Socrates.* You talk rubbish!

*Strepsiades.* Not so, by the gods! if I was dead, no action could lie against me.

*Socrates.* You are merely beating the air. Begone! I will give you no more lessons.

*Strepsiades.* Why not? Oh! Socrates! in the name of the gods!

*Socrates.* But you forget as fast as you learn. Come, what was the thing I taught you first? Tell me.

*Strepsiades.* Ah! let me see. What was the first thing? What was it then? Ah! that thing in which we knead the bread, oh! my god! what do you call it?

*Socrates.* Plague take the most forgetful and silliest of old addlepates!

*Strepsiades.* Alas! what a calamity! what will become of me? I am undone if I do not learn how to ply my tongue. Oh! Clouds! give me good advice.

*Chorus.* Old man, we counsel you, if you have brought up a son, to send him to learn in your stead.

*Strepsiades.* Undoubtedly I have a son, as well endowed as the best, but he is unwilling to learn. What will become of me?

*Chorus.* And you don't make him obey you?

*Strepsiades.* You see, he is big and strong; moreover, through his mother he is a descendant of those fine birds, the race of Coesyra. Nevertheless, I will go and find him, and if he refuses, I will turn him out of the house. Go in, Socrates, and wait for me awhile.

*Chorus (to Socrates).* Do you understand, that, thanks to us, you will be loaded with benefits? Here is a man, ready to obey you in all things. You see how he is carried away with admiration and enthusiasm. Profit by it to clip him as short as possible; fine chances are all too quickly gone.

*Strepsiades.* No, by the Clouds! you stay no longer here; go and devour the ruins of your uncle Megacles' fortune.

*Phidippides.* Oh! my poor father! what has happened to you? By the Olympian Zeus! you are no longer in your senses!

*Strepsiades.* See! see! "the Olympian Zeus." Oh! the fool! to believe in Zeus at your age!

*Phidippides.* What is there in that to make you laugh?

*Strepsiades.* You are then a tiny little child, if you

credit such antiquated rubbish! But come here, that I may teach you; I will tell you something very necessary to know to be a man; but you will not repeat it to anybody.

*Phidippides.* Come, what is it?

*Strepsiades.* Just now you swore by Zeus.

*Phidippides.* Aye, that I did.

*Strepsiades.* Do you see how good it is to learn? Phidippides, there is no Zeus.

*Phidippides.* What is there then?

*Strepsiades.* 'Tis the Whirlwind, that has driven out Jupiter and is King now.

*Phidippides.* Got to! what drivel!

*Strepsiades.* Know it to be the truth.

*Phidippides.* And who says so?

*Strepsiades.* 'Tis Socrates, the Melian, and Chaerephon, who knows how to measure the jump of a flea.

*Phidippides.* Have you reached such a pitch of madness that you believe those bilious fellows?

*Strepsiades.* Use better language, and do not insult men who are clever and full of wisdom, who, to economize, are never shaved, shun the gymnasia and never go to the baths, while you, you only await my death to eat up my wealth. But come, come as quickly as you can to learn in my stead.

*Phidippides.* And what good can be learnt of them?

*Strepsiades.* What good indeed? Why, all human knowledge. Firstly, you will know yourself grossly ignorant. But await me here awhile.

*Phidippides.* Alas! what is to be done? My father has lost his wits. Must I have him certificated for lunacy, or must I order his coffin?

*Strepsiades.* Come! what kind of bird is this? tell me.

*Phidippides.* A pigeon.

*Strepsiades.* Good! And this female?

*Phidippides.* A pigeon.

*Strepsiades.* The same for both? You make me laugh! For the future you will call this one a pigeonnette and the other a pigeon.

*Phidippides.* A pigeonnette! These then are the fine things you have just learnt at the school of these sons of the Earth!

*Strepsiades.* And many others; but what I learnt I forgot at once, because I am too old.

*Phidippides.* So this is why you have lost your cloak?

*Strepsiades.* I have not lost it, I have consecrated it to Philosophy.

*Phidippides.* And what have you done with your sandals, you poor fool?

*Strepsiades.* If I have lost them, it is for what was necessary, just as Pericles did. But come, move yourself, let us go in; if necessary, do wrong to obey your father. When you were six years old and still lisped, 'twas I who obeyed you. I remember at the feasts of Zeus you had a consuming wish for a little chariot and I bought it for you with the first obolus which I received as a juryman in the Courts.

*Phidippides.* You will soon repent of what you ask me to do.

*Strepsiades.* Oh! now I am happy! He obeys. Here, Socrates, here! Come out quick! Here I am bringing you my son; he refused, but I have persuaded him.

*Socrates.* Why, he is but a child yet. He is not used to these baskets, in which we suspend our minds.

*Phidippides.* To make you better used to them, I would you were hung.

*Strepsiades.* A curse upon you! you insult your master!

*Socrates.* "I would you were hung!" What a stupid speech! and so emphatically spoken! How can one ever get out of an accusation with such a tone, summon witnesses or touch or convince? And yet when we think, Hyperbolus learnt all this for one talent!

*Strepsiades.* Rest undisturbed and teach him. 'Tis a most intelligent nature. Even when quite little he amused himself at home with making houses, carving boats, constructing little chariots of leather, and understood wonderfully how to make frogs out of pomegranate rinds. Teach him both methods of reasoning, the strong and also the weak, which by false arguments triumphs over the strong; if not the two, at least the false, and that in every possible way.

*Socrates.* 'Tis Just and Unjust Discourse themselves that shall instruct him.

*Strepsiades.* I go, but forget it not, he must always, always be able to confound the true.

*Just Discourse.* Come here! Shameless as you may be, will you dare to show your face to the spectators?

*Unjust Discourse.* Take me where you list. I seek a throng, so that I may the better annihilate you.

*Just Discourse.* Annihilate me! Do you forget who you are?

*Unjust Discourse.* I am Reasoning.

*Just Discourse.* Yes, the weaker Reasoning.

*Unjust Discourse.* But I triumph over you, who claim to be the stronger.

*Just Discourse.* By what cunning shifts, pray?

*Unjust Discourse.* By the invention of new maxims.

*Just Discourse.* . . . which are received with favour by these fools.

*Unjust Discourse.* Say rather, by these wiseacres.

*Just Discourse.* I am going to destroy you mercilessly.

*Unjust Discourse.* How pray? Let us see you do it.

*Just Discourse.* By saying what is true.

*Unjust Discourse.* I shall retort and shall very soon

have the better of you. First, I maintain that justice has no existence.

*Just Discourse.* Has no existence?

*Unjust Discourse.* No existence! Why, where is it?

*Just Discourse.* With the gods.

*Unjust Discourse.* How then, if justice exists, was Zeus not put to death for having put his father in chains?

*Just Discourse.* Bah! this is enough to turn my stomach! A basin, quick!

*Unjust Discourse.* You are an old driveller and stupid withal.

*Just Discourse.* And you a debauchee and a shameless fellow.

*Unjust Discourse.* Hah! What sweet expressions!

*Just Discourse.* An impious buffoon.

*Unjust Discourse.* You crown me with roses and with lilies.

*Just Discourse.* A parricide.

*Unjust Discourse.* Why, you shower gold upon me.

*Just Discourse.* Formerly, 'twas a hailstorm of blows.

*Unjust Discourse.* I deck myself with your abuse.

*Just Discourse.* What impudence!

*Unjust Discourse.* What tomfoolery!

*Just Discourse.* 'Tis because of you that the youth no longer attends the schools. The Athenians will soon recognize what lessons you teach those who are fools enough to believe you.

*Unjust Discourse.* You are overwhelmed with wretchedness.

*Just Discourse.* And you, you prosper. Yet you were poor when you said, "I am the Mysian Telephus," and used to stuff your wallet with maxims of Pandeletus to nibble at.

*Unjust Discourse.* Oh! the beautiful wisdom, of which you are now boasting!

*Just Discourse.* Madman! But yet madder the city that keeps you, you, the corrupter of its youth!

*Unjust Discourse.* 'Tis not you who will teach this young man; you are as old and out of date as Saturn.

*Just Discourse.* Nay, it will certainly be I, if he does not wish to be lost and to practise verbosity only.

*Unjust Discourse* (*to Phidippides*). Come hither and leave him to beat the air.

*Just Discourse* (*to Unjust Discourse*). Evil be unto you, if you touch him.

*Chorus.* A truce to your quarrellings and abuse! But expound, you, what you taught us formerly, and you, your new doctrine. Thus, after hearing each of you argue, he will be able to choose betwixt the two schools.

*Just Discourse.* I am quite agreeable.

*Unjust Discourse.* And I too.

*Chorus.* Who is to speak first?

*Unjust Discourse.* Let it be my opponent, he has my full consent; then I will follow upon the very ground he shall have chosen and shall shatter him with a hail of new ideas and subtle fancies; if after that he dares to breathe another word, I shall sting him in the face and in the eyes with our maxims, which are as keen as the sting of a wasp, and he will die.

*Chorus.* Here are two rivals confident in their powers of oratory and in the thoughts over which they have pondered so long. Let us see which will come triumphant out of the contest. This wisdom, for which my friends maintain such a persistent fight, is in great danger. Come then, you, who crowned men of other days with so many virtues, plead the cause dear to you, make yourself known to us.

*Just Discourse.* Very well, I will tell you what was the old education, when I used to teach justice with so much success and when modesty was held in veneration.

Firstly, it was required of a child, that it should not utter a word. In the street, when they went to the music-school, all the youths of the same district marched lightly clad and ranged in good order, even when the snow was falling in great flakes. At the master's house they had to stand, their legs apart, and they were taught to sing either, "Pallas, the Terrible, who overturneth cities," or "A noise resounded from afar" in the solemn tones of the ancient harmony. If anyone indulged in buffoonery or lent his voice any of the soft inflexions, like those which to-day the disciples of Phrynis take so much pains to form, he was treated as an enemy of the Muses and belaboured with blows. In the wrestling school they would sit with outstretched legs and without display of any indecency to the curious. When they rose, they would smooth over the sand, so as to leave no trace to excite obscene thoughts. Never was a child rubbed with oil below the belt; the rest of their bodies thus retained its fresh bloom and down, like a velvety peach. They were not to be seen approaching a lover and themselves rousing his passion by soft modulation of the voice and lustful gaze. At table, they would not have dared, before those older than themselves, to have taken a radish, an aniseed or a leaf of parsley, and much less eat fish or thrushes or cross their legs.

*Unjust Discourse.* What antiquated rubbish! Have we got back to the days of the festivals of Zeus Polieus, to the Buphonia, to the time of the poet Cecydes and the golden cicadas?

*Just Discourse.* 'Tis nevertheless by suchlike teaching I built up the men of Marathon. But you, you teach the children of to-day to bundle themselves quickly into their clothes, and I am enraged when I see them at the Panathenaea forgetting Athené while they dance, and covering themselves with their bucklers. Hence, young man, dare to range yourself beside me, who follows justice and truth; you will then be able to shun the public place, to refrain from the baths, to blush at all that is shameful, to fire up if your virtue is mocked at, to give place to your elders, to honour your parents, in short, to avoid all that is evil. Be modesty itself, and do not run to applaud the dancing girls; if you delight in such scenes, some courtesan will cast you her apple and your reputation will be done for. Do not bandy words with your father, nor treat him as a dotard, nor reproach the old man, who has cherished you, with his age.

*Unjust Discourse.* If you listen to him, by Bacchus! you will be the image of the sons of Hippocrates and will be called *mother's great ninny.*

*Just Discourse.* No, but you will pass your days at the gymnasia, glowing with strength and health; you will not go to the public place to cackle and wrangle as is done nowadays; you will not live in fear that you may be dragged before the courts for some trifle exaggerated by quibbling. But you will go down to the Academy to run beneath the sacred olives with some virtuous friend of your own age, your head encircled with the white reed, enjoying your ease and breathing the perfume of the yew and of the fresh sprouts of the poplar, rejoicing in the return of springtide and gladly listening to the gentle rustle of the plane tree and the elm. If you devote yourself to practising my precepts, your chest will be stout, your colour glowing, your shoulders broad, your tongue short, your hips muscular, but your other parts small. But if you follow the fashions of the day, you will be pallid in hue, have narrow shoulders, a narrow chest, a long tongue, small hips and a big thing; you will know how to spin forth long-winded arguments on law. You will be persuaded also to regard as splendid everything that is shameful and as shameful everything that is honourable;

in a word, you will wallow in debauchery like Antimachus.

*Chorus.* How beautiful, high-souled, brilliant is this wisdom that you practise! What a sweet odour of honesty is emitted by your discourse! Happy were those men of other days who lived when you were honoured! And you, seductive talker, come, find some fresh arguments, for your rival has done wonders. Bring out against him all the battery of your wit, if you desire to beat him and not to be laughed out of court.

*Unjust Discourse.* At last! I was choking with impatience, I was burning to upset all his arguments! If I am called the Weaker Reasoning in the schools, 'tis precisely because I was the first before all others to discover the means to confute the laws and the decrees of justice. To invoke solely the weaker arguments and yet triumph is a talent worth more than a hundred thousand drachmae. But see how I shall batter down the sort of education of which he is so proud. Firstly, he forbids you to bathe in hot water. What grounds have you for condemning hot baths?

*Just Discourse.* Because they are baneful and enervate men.

*Unjust Discourse.* Enough said! Oh! you poor wrestler! From the very outset I have seized you and hold you round the middle; you cannot escape me. Tell me, of all the sons of Zeus, who had the stoutest heart, who performed the most doughty deeds?

*Just Discourse.* None, in my opinion, surpassed Heracles.

*Unjust Discourse.* Where have you ever seen cold baths called 'Bath of Heracles'? And yet who was braver than he?

*Just Discourse.* 'Tis because of such quibbles, that the baths are seen crowded with young folk, who chatter there the livelong day while the gymnasia remain empty.

*Unjust Discourse.* Next you condemn the habit of frequenting the market-place, while I approve this. If it were wrong Homer would never have made Nestor speak in public as well as all his wise heroes. As for the art of speaking, he tells you, young men should not practise it; I hold the contrary. Furthermore he preaches chasity to them. Both precepts are equally harmful. Have you ever seen chasity of any use to anyone? Answer and try to confute me.

*Just Discourse.* To many; for instance, Peleus won a sword thereby.

*Unjust Discourse.* A sword! Ah! what a fine present to make him! Poor wretch! Hyperbolus, the lamp-seller, thanks to his villainy, has gained more than . . . I do not know how many talents, but certainly no sword.

*Just Discourse.* Peleus owed it to his chasity that he became the husband of Thetis.

*Unjust Discourse.* . . . who left him in the lurch, for he was not the most ardent; in those nocturnal sports between two sheets, which so please women, he possessed but little merit. Get you gone, you are but an old fool. But you, young man, just consider a little what this temperance means and the delights of which it deprives you—young fellows, women, play, dainty dishes, wine, boisterous laughter. And what is life worth without these? Then, if you happen to commit one of these faults inherent in human weakness, some seduction or adultery, and you are caught in the act, you are lost, if you cannot speak. But follow my teaching and you will be able to satisfy your passions, to dance, to laugh, to blush at nothing. Are you surprised in adultery? Then up and tell the husband you are not guilty, and recall to him the example of Zeus, who allowed himself to be conquered by love and by women. Being but a mortal, can you be stronger than a god?

*Just Discourse.* And if your pupil gets impaled, his hairs plucked out, and he is seared with a hot ember, how are you going to prove to him that he is not a filthy debauchee?

*Unjust Discourse.* And wherein lies the harm of being so?

*Just Discourse.* Is there anything worse than to have such a character?

*Unjust Discourse.* Now what will you say, if I beat you even on this point?

*Just Discourse.* I should certainly have to be silent then.

*Unjust Discourse.* Well then, reply! Our advocates, what are they?

*Just Discourse.* Low scum.

*Unjust Discourse.* Nothing is more true. And our tragic poets?

*Just Discourse.* Low scum.

*Unjust Discourse.* Well said again. And our demagogues?

*Just Discourse.* Low scum.

*Unjust Discourse.* You admit that you have spoken nonsense. And the spectators, what are they for the most part? Look at them.

*Just Discourse.* I am looking at them.

*Unjust Discourse.* Well! What do you see?

*Just Discourse.* By the gods, they are nearly all low scum. See, this one I know to be such and that one and that other with the long hair.

*Unjust Discourse.* What have you to say, then?

*Just Discourse.* I am beaten. Debauchees! in the name of the gods, receive my cloak; I pass over to your ranks.

*Socrates.* Well then! do you take away your son or do you wish me to teach him how to speak?

*Strepsiades.* Teach him, chastise him and do not fail to sharpen his tongue well, on one side for petty law-suits and on the other for important cases.

*Socrates.* Make yourself easy, I shall return to you an accomplished sophist.

*Phidippides.* Very pale then and thoroughly hang-dog-looking.

*Strepsiades.* Take him with you.

*Phidippides.* I do assure you, you will repent it.

*Chorus.* Judges, we are all about to tell you what you will gain by awarding us the crown as equity requires of you. In spring, when you wish to give your fields the first dressing, we will rain upon you first; the others shall wait. Then we will watch over your corn and over your vine-stocks; they will have no excess to fear, neither of heat nor of wet. But if a mortal dares to insult the goddesses of the Clouds, let him think of the ills we shall pour upon him. For him neither wine nor any harvest at all! Our terrible slings will mow down his young olive plants and his vines. If he is making bricks, it will rain, and our round hailstones will break the tiles of his roof. If he himself marries or any of his relations or friends, we shall cause rain to fall the whole night long. Verily, he would prefer to live in Egypt than to have given this iniquitous verdict.

*Strepsiades.* Another four, three, two days, then the eve, then the day, the fatal day of payment! I tremble, I quake, I shudder, for 'tis the day of the old moon and the new. Then all my creditors take the oath, pay their deposits, swear my downfall and my ruin. As for me, I beseech them to be reasonable, to be just, "My friend, do not demand this sum, wait a little for this other and give me time for this third one." Then they will pretend that at this rate they will never be repaid, will accuse me of bad faith and will threaten me with the law. Well then, let them sue me! I care nothing for that, if only Phidippides has learnt to speak fluently. I go to find out, let me knock at the door of the school. . . . Ho! slave, slave!

*Socrates.* Welcome! Strepsiades!

*Strepsiades.* Welcome! Socrates! But first take this sack (*offers him a sack of flour*); it is right to reward the master with some present. And my son, whom you took off lately, has he learnt this famous reasoning, tell me.

*Socrates.* He has learnt it.

*Strepsiades.* What a good thing! Oh! thou divine Knavery!

*Socrates.* You will win just as many causes as you choose.

*Strepsiades.* Even if I have borrowed before witnesses?

*Socrates.* So much the better, even if there are a thousand of 'em!

*Strepsiades.* Then I am going to shout with all my might. "Woe to the usurers, woe to their capital and their interest and their compound interest! You shall play me no more bad turns. My son is being taught there, his tongue is being sharpened into a double-edged weapon; he is my defender, the saviour of my house, the ruin of my foes! His poor father was crushed down with misfortune and he delivers him." Go and call him to me quickly. Oh! my child! my dear little one! run forward to your father's voice!

*Socrates.* Here he is.

*Strepsiades.* Oh, my friend, my dearest friend!

*Socrates.* Take your son, and get you gone.

*Strepsiades.* Oh, my son! oh! oh! what a pleasure to see your pallor! You are ready first to deny and then to contradict; 'tis as clear as noon. What a child of your country you are! How your lips quiver with the famous,

"What have you to say now?" How well you know, I am certain, to put on the look of a victim, when it is you who are making both victims and dupes! and what a truly Attic glance! Come, 'tis for you to save me, seeing it is you who have ruined me.

*Phidippides.* What is it you fear then?

*Strepsiades.* The day of the old and the new.

*Phidippides.* Is there then a day of the old and the new?

*Strepsiades.* The day on which they threaten to pay deposit against me.

*Phidippides.* Then so much the worse for those who have deposited! for 'tis not possible for one day to be two.

*Strepsiades.* What?

*Phidippides.* Why, undoubtedly, unless a woman can be both old and young at the same time.

*Strepsiades.* But so runs the law.

*Phidippides.* I think the meaning of the law is quite misunderstood.

*Strepsiades.* What does it mean?

*Phidippides.* Old Solon loved the people.

*Strepsiades.* What has that to do with the old day and the new?

*Phidippides.* He has fixed two days for the summons, the last day of the old moon and the first day of the new; but the deposits must only be paid on the first day of the new moon.

*Strepsiades.* And why did he also name the last day of the old?

*Phidippides.* So, my dear sir, that the debtors, being there the day before, might free themselves by mutual agreement, or that else, if not, the creditor might begin his action on the morning of the new moon.

*Strepsiades.* Why then do the magistrates have the deposits paid on the last of the month and not the next day?

*Phidippides.* I think they do as the gluttons do, who are the first to pounce upon the dishes. Being eager to carry off their deposits, they have them paid in a day too soon.

*Strepsiades.* Splendid! Ah! poor brutes, who serve for food to us clever folk! You are only down here to swell the number, true blockheads, sheep for shearing, heap of empty pots! Hence I will sound the note of victory for my son and myself. "Oh! happy, Strepsiades! what cleverness is thine! and what a son thou hast here!" Thus my friends and my neighbours will say, jealous at seeing me gain all my suits. But come in, I wish to regale you first.

*Pasias (to his witness).* A man should never lend a single obolus. 'Twould be better to put on a brazen face at the outset than to get entangled in such matters. I want to see my money again and I bring you here to-day to attest the loan. I am going to make a foe of a neighbour; but, as long as I live, I do not wish my country to have to blush for me. Come, I am going to summon Strepsiades.

*Strepsiades.* Who is this?

*Pasias.* . . . for the old day and the new.

*Strepsiades.* I call you to witness, that he has named two days. What do you want of me?

*Pasias.* I claim of you the twelve minae, which you borrowed from me to buy the dapple-grey horse.

*Strepsiades.* A horse! do you hear him? I, who detest horses, as is well known.

*Pasias.* I call Zeus to witness, that you swore by the gods to return them to me.

*Strepsiades.* Because at that time, by Zeus! Phidippides did not yet know the irrefutable argument.

*Pasias.* Would you deny the debt on that account?

*Strepsiades.* If not, what use is his science to me?

*Pasias*. Will you dare to swear by the gods that you owe me nothing?

*Strepsiades*. By which gods?

*Pasias*. By Zeus, Hermes and Posidon!

*Strepsiades*. Why, I would give three obols for the pleasure of swearing by them.

*Pasias*. Woe upon you, impudent knave!

*Strepsiades*. Oh! what a fine wine-skin you would make if flayed!

*Pasias*. Heaven! he jeers at me!

*Strepsiades*. It would hold six gallons easily.

*Pasias*. By great Zeus! by all the gods! you shall not scoff at me with impunity.

*Strepsiades*. Ah! how you amuse me with your gods! how ridiculous it seems to a sage to hear Zeus invoked.

*Pasias*. Your blasphemies will one day meet their reward. But, come, will you repay me my money, yes or no? Answer me, that I may go.

*Strepsiades*. Wait a moment, I am going to give you a distinct answer. (*Goes indoors and returns immediately with a kneading-trough*.)

*Pasias*. What do you think he will do?

*Witness*. He will pay the debt.

*Strepsiades*. Where is the man who demands money? Tell me, what is this?

*Pasias*. Him? Why, he is your kneading-trough.

*Strepsiades*. And you dare to demand money of me, when you are so ignorant? I will not return an obolus to anyone who says *him* instead of *her* for a kneading-trough.

*Pasias*. You will not repay?

*Strepsiades*. Not if I know it. Come, an end to this, pack off as quick as you can.

*Pasias*. I go, but, may I die, if it be not to pay my deposit for a summons.

*Strepsiades.* Very well! 'Twill be so much more to the bad to add to the twelve minae. But truly it makes me sad, for I do pity a poor simpleton who says *him* for a kneading-trough.

*Amynias.* Woe! ah woe is me!

*Strepsiades.* Hold! who is this whining fellow? Can it be one of the gods of Carcinus?

*Amynias.* Do you want to know who I am? I am a man of misfortune!

*Strepsiades.* Get on your way then.

*Amynias.* Oh! cruel god! O Fate, who hath broken the wheels of my chariot! Oh, Pallas, thou hast undone me!

*Strepsiades.* What ill has Tlepolemus done you?

*Amynias.* Instead of jeering me, friend, make your son return me the money he has had of me; I am already unfortunate enough.

*Strepsiades.* What money?

*Amynias.* The money he borrowed of me.

*Strepsiades.* You have indeed had misfortune, it seems to me.

*Amynias.* Yes, by the gods! I have been thrown from a chariot.

*Strepsiades.* Why then drivel as if you had fallen from an ass?

*Amynias.* Am I drivelling because I demand my money?

*Strepsiades.* No, no, you cannot be in your right senses.

*Amynias.* Why?

*Strepsiades.* No doubt your poor wits have had a shake.

*Amynias.* But by Hermes! I will sue you at law, if you do not pay me.

*Strepsiades.* Just tell me; do you think it is always fresh water that Zeus lets fall every time it rains, or is it always the same water that the sun pumps over the earth?

*Amynias.* I neither know, nor care.

*Strepsiades*. And actually you would claim the right to demand your money, when you know not a syllable of these celestial phenomena?

*Amynias*. If you are short, pay me the interest, at any rate.

*Strepsiades*. What kind of animal is interest?

*Amynias*. What? Does not the sum borrowed go on growing, growing every month, each day as the time slips by?

*Strepsiades*. Well put. But do you believe there is more water in the sea now than there was formerly?

*Amynias*. No, 'tis just the same quantity. It cannot increase.

*Strepsiades*. Thus, poor fool, the sea, that receives the rivers, never grows, and yet you would have your money grow? Get you gone, away with you, quick! Ho! bring me the ox-goad!

*Amynias*. Hither! you witnesses there!

*Strepsiades*. Come, what are you waiting for? Will you not budge, old nag!

*Amynias*. What an insult!

*Strepsiades*. Unless you get a-trotting, I shall catch you and prick up your behind, you sorry packhorse! Ah! you start, do you? I was about to drive you pretty fast, I tell you—you and your wheels and your chariot!

*Chorus*. Whither does the passion of evil lead! here is a perverse old man, who wants to cheat his creditors; but some mishap, which will speedily punish this rogue for his shameful schemings, cannot fail to overtake him from to-day. For a long time he has been burning to have his son know how to fight against all justice and right and to gain even the most iniquitous causes against his adversaries every one. I think this wish is going to be fulfilled. But mayhap, mayhap, he will soon wish his son were dumb rather!

*Strepsiades.* Oh! oh! neighbours, kinsmen, fellow-citizens, help! help! to the rescue, I am being beaten! Oh! my head! oh! my jaw! Scoundrel! do you beat your own father!

*Phidippides.* Yes, father, I do.

*Strepsiades.* See! he admits he is beating me.

*Phidippides.* Undoubtedly I do.

*Strepsiades.* You villain, you parricide, you gallows-bird!

*Phidippides.* Go on, repeat your epithets, call me a thousand other names, an it please you. The more you curse, the greater my amusement!

*Strepsiades.* Oh! you infamous cynic!

*Phidippides.* How fragrant the perfume breathed forth in your words.

*Strepsiades.* Do you beat your own father?

*Phidippides.* Aye, by Zeus! and I am going to show you that I do right in beating you.

*Strepsiades.* Oh, wretch! can it be right to beat a father?

*Phidippides.* I will prove it to you, and you shall own yourself vanquished.

*Strepsiades.* Own myself vanquished on a point like this?

*Phidippides.* 'Tis the easiest thing in the world. Choose whichever of the two reasonings you like.

*Strepsiades.* Of which reasonings?

*Phidippides.* The Stronger and the Weaker.

*Strepsiades.* Miserable fellow! Why, 'tis I who had you taught how to refute what is right, and now you would persuade me it is right a son should beat his father.

*Phidippides.* I think I shall convince you so thoroughly that, when you have heard me, you will not have a word to say.

*Strepsiades*. Well, I am curious to hear what you have to say.

*Chorus*. Consider well, old man, how you can best triumph over him. His brazenness shows me that he thinks himself sure of his case; he has some arguments which gives him nerve. Note the confidence in his look! But how did the fight begin? tell the Chorus; you cannot help doing that much.

*Strepsiades*. I will tell you what was the start of the quarrel. At the end of the meal you wot of, I bade him take his lyre and sing me the air of Simonides, which tells of the fleece of the ram. He replied bluntly, that it was stupid, while drinking, to play the lyre and sing, like a woman when she is grinding barley.

*Phidippides*. Why, by rights I ought to have beaten and kicked you the very moment you told me to sing!

*Strepsiades*. That is just how he spoke to me in the house, furthermore he added, that Simonides was a detestable poet. However, I mastered myself and for a while said nothing. Then I said to him, 'At least, take a myrtle branch and recite a passage from Aeschylus to me.'—'For my own part,' he at once replied, 'I look upon Aeschylus as the first of poets, for his verses roll superbly; 'tis nothing but incoherence, bombast and turgidness.' Yet still I smothered my wrath and said, 'Then recite one of the famous pieces from the modern poets.' Then he commenced a piece in which Euripides shows, oh! horror! a brother, who violates his own uterine sister. Then I could no longer restrain myself, and attacked him with the most injurious abuse; naturally he retorted; hard words were hurled on both sides, and finally he sprang at me, broke my bones, bore me to earth, strangled and started killing me!

*Phidippides*. I was right. What! not praise Euripides, the greatest of our poets!

*Strepsiades.* He the greatest of our poets! Ah! if I but dared to speak! but the blows would rain upon me harder than ever.

*Phidippides.* Undoubtedly and rightly too.

*Strepsiades.* Rightly! oh! what impudence! to me, who brought you up! when you could hardly lisp, I guessed what you wanted. If you said *broo, broo,* well, I brought you your milk; if you asked for *mam mam,* I gave you bread; and you had no sooner said, *caca,* than I took you outside and held you out. And just now, when you were strangling me, I shouted, I bellowed that I would let all go; and you, you scoundrel, had not the heart to take me outside, so that here, though almost choking, I was compelled to ease myself.

*Chorus.* Young men, your hearts must be panting with impatience. What is Phidippides going to say? If, after such conduct, he proves he has done well, I would not give an obolus for the hide of old men. Come, you, who know how to brandish and hurl the keen shafts of the new science, find a way to convince us, give your language an appearance of truth.

*Phidippides.* How pleasant it is to know these clever new inventions and to be able to defy the established laws! When I thought only about horses, I was not able to string three words together without a mistake, but now that the master has altered and improved me and that I live in this world of subtle thought, of reasoning and of meditation, I count on being able to prove satisfactorily that I have done well to thrash my father.

*Strepsiades.* Mount your horse! By Zeus! I would rather defray the keep of a four-in-hand team than be battered with blows.

*Phidippides.* I revert to what I was saying when you interrupted me. And first, answer me, did you beat me in my childhood?

*Strepsiades.* Why, assuredly, for your good and in your own best interest.

*Phidippides.* Tell me, is it not right, that in turn I should beat you for your good? since it is for a man's own best interest to be beaten. What! must your body be free of blows, and not mine? am I not free-born too? the children are to weep and the fathers go free?

*Strepsiades.* But . . .

*Phidippides.* You will tell me, that according to the law, 'tis the lot of children to be beaten. But I reply that the old men are children twice over and that it is far more fitting to chastise them than the young, for there is less excuse for their faults.

*Strepsiades.* But the law nowhere admits that fathers should be treated thus.

*Phidippides.* Was not the legislator who carried this law a man like you and me? In those days he got men to believe him; then why should not I too have the right to establish for the future a new law, allowing children to beat their fathers in turn? We make you a present of all the blows which were received before this law, and admit that you thrashed us with impunity. But look how the cocks and other animals fight with their fathers; and yet what difference is there betwixt them and ourselves, unless it be that they do not propose decrees?

*Strepsiades.* But if you imitate the cocks in all things, why don't you scratch up the dunghill, why don't you sleep on a perch?

*Phidippides.* That has no bearing on the case, good sir; Socrates would find no connection, I assure you.

*Strepsiades.* Then do not beat at all, for otherwise you have only yourself to blame afterwards.

*Phidippides.* What for?

*Strepsiades.* I have the right to chastise you, and you to chastise your son, if you have one.

*Phidippides.* And if I have not, I shall have cried in vain, and you will die laughing in my face.

*Strepsiades.* What say you, all here present? It seems to me that he is right, and I am of opinion that they should be accorded their right. If we think wrongly, 'tis but just we should be beaten.

*Phidippides.* Again, consider this other point.

*Strepsiades.* 'Twill be the death of me.

*Phidippides.* But you will certainly feel no more anger because of the blows I have given you.

*Strepsiades.* Come, show me what profit I shall gain from it.

*Phidippides.* I shall beat my mother just as I have you.

*Strepsiades.* What do you say? what's that you say? Hah! this is far worse still.

*Phidippides.* And what if I prove to you by our school reasoning, that one ought to beat one's mother?

*Strepsiades.* Ah! if you do that, then you will only have to throw yourself, along with Socrates and his reasoning, into the Barathrum. Oh! Clouds! all our troubles emanate from you, from you, to whom I entrusted myself, body and soul.

*Chorus.* No, you alone are the cause, because you have pursued the path of evil.

*Strepsiades.* Why did you not say so then, instead of egging on a poor ignorant old man?

*Chorus.* We always act thus, when we see a man conceive a passion for what is evil; we strike him with some terrible disgrace, so that he may learn to fear the gods.

*Strepsiades.* Alas! oh Clouds! 'tis hard indeed, but 'tis just! I ought not to have cheated my creditors. . . . But come, my dear son, come with me to take vengeance on this wretched Chaerephon and on Socrates, who have deceived us both.

*Phidippides.* I shall do nothing against our masters.

*Strepsiades.* Oh! show some reverence for ancestral Zeus!

*Phidippides.* Mark him and his ancestral Zeus! What a fool you are! Does any such being as Zeus exist?

*Strepsiades.* Why, assuredly.

*Phidippides.* No, a thousand times no! The ruler of the world is the Whirlwind, that has unseated Zeus.

*Strepsiades.* He has not dethroned him. I believe it, because of this whirligig here. Unhappy wretch that I am! I have taken a piece of clay to be a god.

*Phidippides.* Very well! Keep your stupid nonsense for your own consumption. (*Exit.*)

*Strepsiades.* Oh! what madness! I had lost my reason when I threw over the gods through Socrates' seductive phrases. Oh! good Hermes, do not destroy me in your wrath. Forgive me; their babbling had driven me crazy. Be my councillor. Shall I pursue them at law or shall I . . . ? Order and I obey.—You are right, no law-suit; but up! let us burn down the home of those praters. Here, Xanthias, here! take a ladder, come forth and arm yourself with an axe; now mount upon the school, demolish the roof, if you love your master, and may the house fall in upon them. Ho! bring me a blazing torch! There is more than one of them, arch-impostors as they are, on whom I am determined to have vengeance.

*A Disciple.* Oh! oh!

*Strepsiades.* Come, torch, do your duty! Burst into full flame!

*Disciple.* What are you up to?

*Strepsiades.* What am I up to? Why, I am entering upon a subtle argument with the beams of the house.

*Second Disciple.* Hullo! hullo! who is burning down our house?

*Strepsiades.* The man whose cloak you have appropriated.

*Second Disciple*. But we are dead men, dead men!

*Strepsiades*. That is just exactly what I hope, unless my axe plays me false, or I fall and break my neck.

*Socrates*. Hi! you fellow on the roof, what are you doing up there?

*Strepsiades*. I traverse the air and contemplate the sun.

*Socrates*. Ah! ah! woe is upon me! I am suffocating!

*Chaerephon*. Ah! you insulted the gods! Ah! you studied the face of the moon! Chase them, strike and beat them down! Forward! they have richly deserved their fate—above all, by reason of their blasphemies.

*Chorus*. So let the Chorus file off the stage. Its part is played.

# THE ACHARNIANS

# THE ACHARNIANS

## *Dramatis Personae*

DICAEOPOLIS
HERALD
AMPHITHEUS
AMBASSADORS
PSEUDARTABAS
THEORUS
DAUGHTER OF DICAEOPOLIS
SLAVE OF EURIPIDES
EURIPIDES
LAMACHUS
A MEGARIAN
TWO YOUNG GIRLS, *daughters of the Megarian*
AN INFORMER
A BOEOTIAN
NICARCHUS
SLAVE OF LAMACHUS
A HUSBANDMAN
A WEDDING GUEST
CHORUS OF ACHARNIAN CHARCOAL BURNERS

SCENE: The Orchestra represents the Pnyx at
      Athens; in the background are the usual
      houses, this time three in number, be-
      longing to Dicaeopolis, Euripides, and
      Lamachus respectively.

# THE ACHARNIANS

*Dicaeopolis.* What cares have not gnawed at my heart and how few have been the pleasures in my life! Four, to be exact, while my troubles have been as countless as the grains of sand on the shore! Let me see! of what value to me have been these few pleasures? Ah! I remember that I was delighted in soul when Cleon had to cough up those five talents; I was in ecstasy and I love the Knights for this deed; "it is an honour to Greece." But the day when I was impatiently awaiting a piece by Aeschylus, what tragic despair it caused me when the herald called, "Theognis, introduce your Chorus!" Just imagine how this blow struck straight at my heart! On the other hand, what joy Dexitheus caused me at the musical competition, when right after Moschus he played a Boeotian melody on the lyre! But this year by contrast! Oh! what deadly torture to hear Chaeris perform the prelude in the Orthian mode!—Never, however, since I began to bathe, has the dust hurt my eyes as it does to-day. Still it is the day of assembly; all should be here at daybreak, and yet the Pnyx is still deserted. They are gossiping in the market-place, slipping hither and thither to avoid the vermilioned rope. The Prytanes even do not

come; they will be late, but when they come they will
push and fight each other for a seat in the front row.
They will never trouble themselves with the question of
peace. Oh! Athens! Athens! As for myself, I do not fail
to come here before all the rest, and now, finding myself
alone, I groan, yawn, stretch, fart, and know not what
to do; I make sketches in the dust, pull out my loose hairs,
muse, think of my fields, long for peace, curse town life
and regret my dear country home, which never told me
to "buy fuel, vinegar or oil"; there the word "buy," which
cuts me in two, was unknown; I harvested everything at
will. Therefore I have come to the assembly fully prepared to bawl, interrupt and abuse the speakers, if they
talk of anything but peace. (*The Orchestra begins to fill
with people.*) But here come the Prytanes, and high
time too, for it is midday! There, just as I said, they are
pushing and fighting for the front seats.

*Herald.* Step forward, step forward; get within the
consecrated area.

*Amphitheus.* Has anyone spoken yet?

*Herald.* Who asks to speak?

*Amphitheus.* I do.

*Herald.* Your name?

*Amphitheus.* Amphitheus.

*Herald.* Are you not a man?

*Amphitheus.* No! I am an immortal! Amphitheus was
the son of Ceres and Triptolemus; of him was born Celeus, Celeus wedded Phaenereté, my grandmother, whose
son was Lycinus, and, being born of him I am an immortal; it is to me alone that the gods have entrusted the
duty of treating with the Lacedaemonians. But, citizens,
though I am immortal, I am dying of hunger; the Prytanes give me nothing.

*Herald.* Officers!

*Amphitheus* (*as the Scythian policemen seize him*).

Oh, Triptolemus and Celeus, do ye thus forsake your own blood?

*Dicaeopolis* (*rising*). Prytanes, in expelling this citizen, you are offering an outrage to the Assembly. He only desired to secure peace for us and to sheathe the sword. (*The Scythians release Amphitheus.*)

*Herald.* Sit down! Silence!

*Dicaeopolis.* No, by Apollo, I will not, unless you are going to discuss the question of peace.

*Herald.* The ambassadors, who are returned from the Court of the King!

*Dicaeopolis.* Of what King? I am sick of all those fine birds, the peacock ambassadors and their swagger.

*Herald.* Silence!

*Dicaeopolis* (*as he perceives the entering ambassadors dressed in the Persian mode*). Oh! oh! By Ecbatana, what a costume!

*Ambassador.* During the archonship of Euthymenes, you sent us to the Great King on a salary of two drachmae per diem.

*Dicaeopolis.* Ah! those poor drachmae!

*Ambassador.* We suffered horribly on the plains of the Cayster, sleeping under a tent, stretched deliciously on fine chariots, half dead with weariness.

*Dicaeopolis.* And I was very much at ease, lying on the straw along the battlements!

*Ambassador.* Everywhere we were well received and forced to drink delicious wine out of golden or crystal flagons. . . .

*Dicaeopolis.* Oh, city of Cranaus, thy ambassadors are laughing at thee!

*Ambassador.* For great feeders and heavy drinkers are alone esteemed as men by the barbarians.

*Dicaeopolis.* Just as here in Athens, we only esteem the wenchers and pederasts.

*Ambassador.* At the end of the fourth year we reached the King's Court, but he had left with his whole army to take a crap, and for the space of eight months he was thus sitting on the can in the midst of the golden mountains.

*Dicaeopolis.* And how long did it take him to close his arse? A month?

*Ambassador.* After this he returned to his palace; then he entertained us and had us served with oxen roasted whole in an oven.

*Dicaeopolis.* Who ever saw an ox roasted in an oven? What a lie!

*Ambassador.* And one day, by Zeus, he also had us served with a bird three times as large as Cleonymus, and called the Hoax.

*Dicaeopolis.* And do we give you two drachmae, that you should hoax us thus?

*Ambassador.* We are bringing to you Pseudartabas, the King's Eye.

*Dicaeopolis.* I would a crow might pluck out yours with his beak, you cursed ambassador!

*Herald.* The King's Eye!

(*Enter Pseudartabas, in Persian costume; his mask is one great eye; he is accompanied by two eunuchs.*)

*Dicaeopolis.* Good God! Friend, with your great eye, round like the hole through which the oarsman passes his sweep, you have the air of a galley doubling a cape to gain port.

*Ambassador.* Come, Pseudartabas, give forth the message for the Athenians with which you were charged by the Great King.

*Pseudartabas.* I ártamáne Xárxas ápiaóna satrá.

*Ambassador.* Do you understand what he says?

*Dicaeopolis.* God, no!

*Ambassador.* He says that the Great King will send you gold. (*to Pseudartabas.*) Come, utter the word 'gold' louder and more distinctly.

*Pseudartabas.* Thou shalt not have gold, thou gaping-arsed Ionian.

*Dicaeopolis.* Ah! God help us, but *that's* clear enough!

*Ambassador.* What does he say?

*Dicaeopolis.* That the Ionians are gaping-arsed, if they expect to receive gold from the barbarians.

*Ambassador.* Not so, he speaks of bushels of gold.

*Dicaeopolis.* What bushels? You're nothing but a windbag; get out of the way; I will find out the truth by myself. (*to Pseudartabas.*) Come now, answer me clearly, if you do not wish me to dye your skin red. Will the Great King send us gold? (*Pseudartabas makes a negative sign.*) Then our ambassadors are seeking to deceive us? (*Pseudartabas signs affirmatively.*) These fellows make signs like any Greek; I am sure that they are nothing but Athenians. Oh! ho! I recognize one of these eunuchs; it is Clisthenes, the son of Sibyrtius. Behold the effrontery of this shaven and provocative arse! How, you big baboon, with such a beard do you seek to play the eunuch to us? And this other one? Is it not Straton?

*Herald.* Silence! Sit down! The Senate invites the King's Eye to the Prytaneum.

(*The Ambassadors and Pseudartabas depart.*)

*Dicaeopolis.* Is this not sufficient to drive a man to hang himself? Here I stand chilled to the bone, whilst the doors of the Prytaneum fly wide open to lodge such rascals. But I will do something great and bold. Where is Amphitheus? Come and speak with me.

*Amphitheus.* Here I am.

*Dicaeopolis.* Take these eight drachmae and go and conclude a truce with the Lacedaemonians for me, my wife and my children; I leave you free, my dear Prytanes, to send out embassies and to stand gaping in the air.

(*Amphitheus rushes out.*)

*Herald.* Bring in Theorus, who has returned from the Court of Sitalces.

*Theorus* (*rising; he wears a Thracian costume*). I am here.

*Dicaeopolis.* Another humbug!

*Theorus.* We should not have remained long in Thrace . . .

*Dicaeopolis.* . . . if you had not been well paid.

*Theorus.* . . . if the country had not been covered with snow; the rivers were ice-bound . . .

*Dicaeopolis.* That was when Theognis produced his tragedy.

*Theorus.* . . . during the whole of that time I was holding my own with Sitalces, cup in hand; and, in truth, he adored you to such a degree that he wrote on the walls, "How beautiful are the Athenians!" His son, to whom we gave the freedom of the city, burned with desire to come here and eat sausages at the feast of the Apaturia; he prayed his father to come to the aid of his new country and Sitalces swore on his goblet that he would succour us with such a host that the Athenians would exclaim, "What a cloud of grasshoppers!'"

*Dicaeopolis.* Damned if I believe a word of what you tell us! Excepting the grasshoppers, there is not a grain of truth in it all!

*Theorus.* And he has sent you the most warlike soldiers of all Thrace.

*Dicaeopolis.* Now we shall begin to see clearly.

*Herald.* Come hither, Thracians, whom Theorus brought.

*(A few Thracians are ushered in; they have a most un-
warlike appearance.)*

*Dicaeopolis.* What plague have we here?

*Theorus.* The host of the Odomanti.

*Dicaeopolis.* Of the Odomanti? Tell me what it means.
Who sliced their tools like that?

*Theorus.* If they are given a wage of two drachmae,
they will put all Boeotia to fire and sword.

*Dicaeopolis.* Two drachmae to those circumcised
hounds! Groan aloud, ye people of rowers, bulwark of
Athens! *(The Odomanti steal his sack.)* Ah! great gods!
I am undone; these Odomanti are robbing me of my
garlic! Give me back my garlic.

*Theorus.* Oh! wretched man! do not go near them; they
have eaten garlic.

*Dicaeopolis.* Prytanes, will you let me be treated in
this manner, in my own country and by barbarians? But
I oppose the discussion of paying a wage to the Thracians; I announce an omen; I have just felt a drop of
rain.

*Herald.* Let the Thracians withdraw and return the
day after tomorrow; the Prytanes declare the sitting at
an end.

*(All leave except Dicaeopolis.)*

*Dicaeopolis.* Ye gods, what garlic I have lost! But here
comes Amphitheus returned from Lacedaemon. Welcome, Amphitheus.

*(Amphitheus enters, very much out of breath.)*

*Amphitheus.* No, there is no welcome for me and I fly
as fast as I can, for I am pursued by the Acharnians.

*Dicaeopolis.* Why, what has happened?

*Amphitheus.* I was hurrying to bring your treaty of

truce, but some old dotards from Acharnae got scent of
the thing; they are veterans of Marathon, tough as oak
or maple, of which they are made for sure—rough and
ruthless. They all started shouting: "Wretch! you are the
bearer of a treaty, and the enemy has only just cut our
vines!" Meanwhile they were gathering stones in their
cloaks, so I fled and they ran after me shouting.

*Dicaeopolis.* Let 'em shout as much as they please! But
have you brought me a treaty?

*Amphitheus.* Most certainly, here are three samples to
select from, this one is five years old; taste it.

*Dicaeopolis.* Faugh!

*Amphitheus.* What's the matter?

*Dicaeopolis.* I don't like it; it smells of pitch and of the
ships they are fitting out.

*Amphitheus.* Here is another, ten years old; taste it.

*Dicaeopolis.* It smells strongly of the delegates, who
go around the towns to chide the allies for their slowness.

*Amphitheus.* This last is a truce of thirty years, both
on sea and land.

*Dicaeopolis.* Oh! by Bacchus! what a bouquet! It has
the aroma of nectar and ambrosia; this does not say to
us, "Provision yourselves for three days." But it lisps the
gentle numbers. "Go whither you will." I accept it, ratify
it, drink it at one draught and consign the Acharnians
to limbo. Freed from the war and its ills, I shall celebrate
the rural Dionysia.

*Amphitheus.* And I shall run away, for I'm mortally
afraid of the Acharnians.

(*Amphitheus runs off. Dicaeopolis goes into his house,
carrying his truce. The Chorus of Acharnian Charcoal
Burners enters, in great haste and excitement.*)

*Leader of the Chorus.* This way all! Let us follow our
man; we will demand him of everyone we meet; the pub-

lic weal makes his seizure imperative. Ho, there! tell me which way the bearer of the truce has gone.

*Chorus.* He has escaped us, he has disappeared. Damn old age! When I was young, in the days when I followed Phayllus, running with a sack of coals on my back, this wretch would not have eluded my pursuit, let him be as swift as he will.

*Leader of the Chorus.* But now my limbs are stiff; old Lacratides feels his legs are weighty and the traitor escapes me. No, no, let us follow him; old Acharnians like ourselves shall not be set at naught by a scoundrel . . .

*Chorus.* . . . who has dared, by Zeus, to conclude a truce when I wanted the war continued with double fury in order to avenge my ruined lands. No mercy for our foes until I have pierced their hearts like a sharp reed, so that they dare never again ravage my vineyards.

*Leader of the Chorus.* Come, let us seek the rascal; let us look everywhere, carrying our stones in our hands; let us' hunt him from place to place until we trap him; I could never, never tire of the delight of stoning him.

*Dicaeopolis.* Peace! profane men!

*Leader of the Chorus.* Silence all! Friends, do you hear the sacred formula? Here is he, whom we seek! This way, all! Get out of his way, surely he comes to offer an oblation.

(*The Chorus withdraws to one side.*)

*Dicaeopolis* (*comes out with a pot in his hand; he is followed by his wife, his daughter, who carries a basket, and two slaves*).

Peace, profane men! Let the basket-bearer come for-

ward, and thou, Xanthias, hold the phallus well upright.
Daughter, set down the basket and let us begin the sacrifice.

*Daughter of Dicaeopolis (putting down the basket
and taking out the sacred cake).*

Mother, hand me the ladle, that I may spread the sauce
on the cake.

*Dicaeopolis.* It is well! Oh, mighty Bacchus, it is with
joy that, freed from military duty, I and all mine perform
this solemn rite and offer thee this sacrifice; grant that
I may keep the rural Dionysia without hindrance and
that this truce of thirty years may be propitious for me.
Come, my child, carry the basket gracefully and with a
grave, demure face. Happy he who shall be your posses-
sor and embrace you so firmly at dawn, that you fart
like a weasel. Go forward, and have a care they don't
snatch your jewels in the crowd. Xanthias, walk behind
the basket-bearer and hold the phallus well erect; I will
follow, singing the Phallic hymn; thou, wife, look on
from the top of the terrace. Forward! (*He sings.*)

Oh, Phalés, companion of the orgies of Bacchus,
night reveller, god of adultery and of pederasty,
these past six years I have not been able to invoke
thee. With what joy I return to my farmstead, thanks
to the truce I have concluded, freed from cares, from
fighting and from Lamachuses! How much sweeter,
oh Phalés, Phalés, is it to surprise Thratta, the pretty
woodmaid, Strymodorus' slave, stealing wood from
Mount Phelleus, to catch her under the arms, to
throw her on the ground and lay her, oh, Phalés,
Phalés! If thou wilt drink and bemuse thyself with
me, we shall to-morrow consume some good dish in

honour of the peace, and I will hang up my buckler over the smoking hearth.

(*The procession reaches the place where the Chorus is hiding.*)

*Leader of the Chorus.* That's the man himself. Stone him, stone him, stone him, strike the wretch. All, all of you, pelt him, pelt him!

*Dicaeopolis* (*using his pot for a shield*). What is this? By Heracles, you will smash my pot.

(*The daughter and the two slaves retreat.*)

*Chorus.* It is you that we are stoning, you miserable scoundrel.

*Dicaeopolis.* And for what sin, Acharnian elders, tell me that!

*Chorus.* You ask that, you impudent rascal, traitor to your country; you alone amongst us all have concluded a truce, and you dare to look us in the face!

*Dicaeopolis.* But you do not know *why* I have treated for peace. Listen!

*Chorus.* Listen to you? No, no, you are about to die, we will annihilate you with our stones.

*Dicaeopolis.* But first of all, listen. Stop, my friends.

*Chorus.* I will hear nothing; do not address me; I hate you more than I do Cleon, whom one day I shall flay to make sandals for the Knights. Listen to your long speeches, after you have treated with the Laconians? No, I will punish you.

*Dicaeopolis.* Friends, leave the Laconians out of debate and consider only whether I have not done well to conclude my truce.

*Leader of the Chorus.* Done well! when you have

treated with a people who know neither gods nor truth, nor faith.

*Dicaeopolis.* We attribute too much to the Laconians; as for myself, I know that they are not the cause of all our troubles.

*Leader of the Chorus.* Oh, indeed, rascal! You dare to use such language to me and then expect me to spare you!

*Dicaeopolis.* No, no, they are not the cause of all our troubles, and I who address you claim to be able to prove that they have much to complain of in us.

*Leader of the Chorus.* This passes endurance; my heart bounds with fury. Thus you dare to defend our enemies.

*Dicaeopolis.* Were my head on the block I would uphold what I say and rely on the approval of the people.

*Leader of the Chorus.* Comrades, let us hurl our stones and dye this fellow purple.

*Dicaeopolis.* What black fire-brand has inflamed your heart! You will not hear me? You really will not, Acharnians?

*Leader of the Chorus.* No, a thousand times, no.

*Dicaeopolis.* This is a hateful injustice.

*Leader of the Chorus.* May I die if I listen.

*Dicaeopolis.* Nay, nay! have mercy, have mercy, Acharnians.

*Leader of the Chorus.* You shall die.

*Dicaeopolis.* Well, blood for blood! I will kill your dearest friend. I have here the hostages of Acharnae; I shall disembowel them. (*He goes into the house.*)

*Leader of the Chorus.* Acharnians, what means this threat? Has he got one of our children in his house? What gives him such audacity?

*Dicaeopolis (coming out again).* Stone me, if it please you; I shall avenge myself on this. (*He shows them a basket.*) Let us see whether you have any love for your coals.

*Leader of the Chorus.* Great Gods! this basket is our fellow-citizen. Stop, stop, in heaven's name!

*Dicaeopolis.* I shall dismember it despite your cries; I will listen to nothing.

*Chorus.* How, will you kill this coal-basket, my beloved comrade?

*Dicaeopolis.* Just now you would not listen to me.

*Chorus.* Well, speak now, if you will; tell us, tell us you have a weakness for the Lacedaemonians. I consent to anything; never will I forsake this dear little basket.

*Dicaeopolis.* First, throw down your stones.

*Chorus.* There! it's done. And you put away your sword.

*Dicaeopolis.* Let me see that no stones remain concealed in your cloaks.

*Chorus.* They are all on the ground; see how we shake our garments. Come, no haggling, lay down your sword; we threw away everything while crossing from one side of the Orchestra to the other.

*Dicaeopolis.* What cries of anguish you would have uttered had these coals of Parnes been dismembered, and yet it came very near it; had they perished, their death would have been due to the folly of their fellow-citizens. The poor basket was so frightened, look, it has shed a thick black dust over me, the same as a cuttle-fish does. What an irritable temper! You shout and throw stones, you will not hear my arguments—not even when I propose to speak in favour of the Lacedaemonians with my head on the block, and yet I cling to life. (*He goes into the house.*)

191

*Chorus.* Well then, bring out a block before your door, scoundrel, and let us hear the good grounds you can give us; I am curious to know them. Now mind, as you proposed yourself, place your head on the block and speak.

*Dicaeopolis* (*coming out of his house, carrying a block*). Here is the block; and, though I am but a very sorry speaker, I wish nevertheless to talk freely of the Lacedaemonians and without the protection of my buckler. Yet I have many reasons for fear. I know our rustics; they are delighted if some braggart comes, and rightly or wrongly, loads both them and their city with praise and flattery; they do not see that such toad-eaters are traitors, who sell them for gain. As for the old men, I know their weakness; they only seek to overwhelm the accused with their votes. Nor have I forgotten how Cleon treated me because of my comedy last year; he dragged me before the Senate and there he uttered endless slanders against me; it was a tempest of abuse, a deluge of lies. Through what a slough of mud he dragged me! I almost perished. Permit me, therefore, before I speak, to dress in the manner most likely to draw pity.

*Chorus.* What evasions, subterfuges and delays! Wait! here is the sombre helmet of Pluto with its thick bristling plume; Hieronymus lends it to you; then open Sisyphus' bag of wiles; but hurry, hurry, for our discussion does not admit of delay.

*Dicaeopolis.* The time has come for me to manifest my courage, so I will go and seek Euripides. (*Knocking on Euripides' door.*) Ho! slave, slave!
*Slave.* Who's there?
*Dicaeopolis.* Is Euripides at home?
*Slave.* He is and he isn't; understand that, if you can.

*Dicaeopolis.* What's that? He is and he *isn't!*

*Slave.* Certainly, old man; busy gathering subtle fancies here and there, his mind is not in the house, but he himself is; perched aloft, he is composing a tragedy.

*Dicaeopolis.* Oh, Euripides, you are indeed happy to have a slave so quick at repartee! Now, fellow, call your master.

*Slave.* Impossible! (*He slams the door.*)

*Dicaeopolis.* Too bad. But I will not give up. Come, let us knock at the door again. Euripides, my little Euripides, my darling Euripides, listen; never had man greater right to your pity. It is Dicaeopolis of the Chollidan Deme who calls you. Do you hear?

*Euripides (from within).* I have no time to waste.

*Dicaeopolis.* Very well, have yourself wheeled out here.

*Euripides.* Impossible.

*Dicaeopolis.* Nevertheless . . .

*Euripides.* Well, let them roll me out; as to coming down, I have not the time.

(*The eccyclema turns and presents the interior of the house. Euripides is lying on a bed, his slave beside him. On the back wall are hung up tragic costumes of every sort and a multitude of accessories is piled up on the floor.*)

*Dicaeopolis.* Euripides . . .

*Euripides.* What words strike my ear?

*Dicaeopolis.* You perch aloft to compose tragedies, when you might just as well do them on the ground. No wonder you introduce cripples on the stage. And why do you dress in these miserable tragic rags? No wonder your heroes are beggars. But, Euripides, on my knees I beseech you, give me the tatters of some old piece; for I have to treat the Chorus to a long speech, and if I do it badly it is all over with me.

*Euripides.* What rags do you prefer? Those in which I rigged out Oeneus on the stage, that unhappy, miserable old man?

*Dicaeopolis.* No, I want those of some hero still more unfortunate.

*Euripides.* Of Phoenix, the blind man?

*Dicaeopolis.* No, not of Phoenix, you have another hero more unfortunate than him.

*Euripides.* Now, what tatters *does* he want? (*to Dicaeopolis.*) Do you mean those of the beggar Philoctetes?

*Dicaeopolis.* No, of another far more beggarly.

*Euripides.* Is it the filthy dress of the lame fellow, Bellerophon?

*Dicaeopolis.* No, not Bellerophon; the one I mean was not only lame and a beggar, but boastful and a fine speaker.

*Euripides.* Ah! I know, it is Telephus, the Mysian.

*Dicaeopolis.* Yes, Telephus. Give me his rags, I beg of you.

*Euripides.* Slave! give him Telephus' tatters; they are on top of the rags of Thyestes and mixed with those of Ino. There they are; take them.

*Dicaeopolis* (*holding up the costume for the audience to see*). Oh! Zeus, whose eye pierces everywhere and embraces all, permit me to assume the most wretched dress on earth. Euripides, cap your kindness by giving me the little Mysian hat, that goes so well with these tatters. I must to-day have the look of a beggar; "be what I am, but not appear to be"; the audience will know well who I am, but the Chorus will be fools enough not to, and I shall dupe them with my subtle phrases.

*Euripides.* I will give you the hat; I love the clever tricks of an ingenious brain like yours.

*Dicaeopolis.* Rest happy, and may it befall Telephus as

I wish. Ah, I already feel myself filled with quibbles. But I must have a beggar's staff.

*Euripides (handing him a staff).* Here you are, and now get away from this porch.

*Dicaeopolis.* Oh, my soul! You see how you are driven from this house, when I still need so many accessories. But let us be pressing, obstinate, importunate. Euripides, give me a little basket with a lamp lighted inside.

*Euripides.* Whatever do you want such a thing as that for?

*Dicaeopolis.* I do not need it, but I want it all the same.

*Euripides (handing him a basket).* You importune me; get out of here!

*Dicaeopolis.* Alas! may the gods grant you a destiny as brilliant as your mother's.

*Euripides.* Leave me in peace.

*Dicaeopolis.* Oh, just a little broken cup.

*Euripides (handing him a cup).* Take it and go and hang yourself. *(to himself.)* What a tiresome fellow!

*Dicaeopolis.* Ah! you do not know all the pain you cause me. Dear, good Euripides, just a little pot with a sponge for a stopper.

*Euripides.* Miserable man! You are stealing a whole tragedy. Here, take it and be off. *(He hands Dicaeopolis a pot.)*

*Dicaeopolis.* I am going, but, great gods! I need one thing more; unless I have it, I am a dead man. Hearken, my little Euripides, only give me this and I go, never to return. For pity's sake, do give me a few small herbs for my basket.

*Euripides.* You wish to ruin me then. Here, take what you want; but it is all over with my plays! *(He hands him some herbs.)*

*Dicaeopolis.* I won't ask another thing; I'm going. I am too importunate and forget that I rouse against me the hate of kings. (*He starts to leave, then returns quickly.*) Ah! wretch that I am! I am lost! I have forgotten one thing, without which all the rest is as nothing. Euripides, my excellent Euripides, my dear little Euripides, may I die if I ask you again for the smallest present; only one, the last, absolutely the last; give me some of the chervil your mother left you in her will.

*Euripides.* Insolent hound! Slave, lock the door!

*Dicaeopolis.* Oh, my soul! we must go away without the chervil. Art thou sensible of the dangerous battle we are about to engage upon in defending the Lacédaemonians? Courage, my soul, we must plunge into the midst of it. Does thou hesitate and art thou fully steeped in Euripides? That's right! do not falter, my poor heart, and let us risk our head to say what we hold for truth. Courage and boldly to the front. I am astonished at my bravery. (*He approaches the block.*)

> *Chorus.* What do you purport doing? what are you going to say? What an impudent fellow! what a brazen heart! to dare to stake his head and uphold an opinion contrary to that of us all! And he does not tremble to face this peril! Come, it is you who desired it, speak!

*Dicaeopolis.* Spectators, be not angered if, although I am a beggar, I dare in a comedy to speak before the people of Athens of the public weal; even Comedy can sometimes discern what is right. I shall not please, but I shall say what is true. Besides, Cleon shall not be able to accuse me of attacking Athens before strangers; we are by ourselves at the festival of the Lenaea; the time when our allies send us their tribute and their soldiers is not yet here. There is only the pure wheat without the chaff; as to the resident aliens settled among us, they and the citizens are one, like the straw and the ear.

I detest the Lacedaemonians with all my heart, and
may Posidon, the god of Taenarus, cause an earthquake
and overturn their dwellings! My vines too have been
cut. But come (there are only friends who hear me), why
accuse the Laconians of all our woes? Some men (I do
not say the city, note particularly that I do not say the
city), some wretches, lost in vices, bereft of honour, who
were not even citizens of good stamp, but strangers, have
accused the Megarians of introducing their produce
fraudulently, and not a cucumber, a leveret, a suckling
pig, a clove of garlic, a lump of salt was seen without its
being said, "Halloa! these come from Megara," and their
being instantly confiscated. Thus far the evil was not
serious and we were the only sufferers. But now some
young drunkards go to Megara and carry off the harlot
Simaetha; the Megarians, hurt to the quick, run off in
turn with two harlots of the house of Aspasia; and so
for three whores Greece is set ablaze. Then Pericles,
aflame with ire on his Olympian height, let loose the
lightning, caused the thunder to roll, upset Greece and
passed an edict, which ran like the song, "That the Megarians be banished both from our land and from our
markets and from the sea and from the continent."
Meanwhile the Megarians, who were beginning to die
of hunger, begged the Lacedaemonians to bring about
the abolition of the decree, of which those harlots were
the cause; several times we refused their demand; and
from that time there was a horrible clatter of arms everywhere. You will say that Sparta was wrong, but what
should she have done? Answer that. Suppose that a
Lacedaemonian had seized a little Seriphian dog on any
pretext and had sold it, would you have endured it quietly? Far from it, you would at once have sent three
hundred vessels to sea, and what an uproar there would
have been through all the city! there it's a band of noisy

soldiery, here a brawl about the election of a Trierarch; elsewhere pay is being distributed, the Pallas figure-heads are being regilded, crowds are surging under the market porticos, encumbered with wheat that is being measured, wine-skins, oar-leathers, garlic, olives, onions in nets; everywhere are chaplets, sprats, flute-girls, black eyes; in the arsenal bolts are being noisily driven home, sweeps are being made and fitted with leathers; we hear nothing but the sound of whistles, of flutes and fifes to encourage the workers. That is what you assuredly would have done, and would not Telephus have done the same? So I come to my general conclusion; we have no common sense.

*Leader of First Semi-Chorus.* Oh! wretch! oh! infamous man! You are naught but a beggar and yet you dare to talk to us like this! you insult their worships the informers!

*Leader of Second Semi-Chorus.* By Posidon! he speaks the truth; he has not lied in a single detail.

*Leader of First Semi-Chorus.* But though it be true, need he say it? But you'll have no great cause to be proud of your insolence!

*Leader of Second Semi-Chorus.* Where are you running to? Don't you move; if you strike this man, I shall be at you.

*First Semi-Chorus.* Oh! Lamachus, whose glance flashes lightning, whose plume petrifies thy foes, help! Oh! Lamachus, my friend, the hero of my tribe and all of you, both officers and soldiers, defenders of our walls, come to my aid; else is it all over with me!

(*Lamachus comes out of his house armed from head to foot.*)

*Lamachus.* Whence comes this cry of battle? where must I bring my aid? where must I sow dread? who wants me to uncase my dreadful Gorgon's head?

*Dicaeopolis.* Oh, Lamachus, great hero! Your plumes and your cohorts terrify me.

*Chorus-Leader.* This man, Lamachus, incessantly abuses Athens.

*Lamachus.* You are but a mendicant and you dare to use language of this sort?

*Dicaeopolis.* Oh, brave Lamachus, forgive a beggar who speaks at hazard.

*Lamachus.* But what have you said? Let us hear.

*Dicaeopolis.* I know nothing about it; the sight of weapons makes me dizzy. Oh! I adjure you, take that fearful Gorgon somewhat farther away.

*Lamachus.* There.

*Dicaeopolis.* Now place it face downwards on the ground.

*Lamachus.* It is done.

*Dicaeopolis.* Give me a plume out of your helmet.

*Lamachus.* Here is a feather.

*Dicaeopolis.* And hold my head while I vomit; the plumes have turned my stomach.

*Lamachus.* Hah! what are you proposing to do? do you want to make yourself vomit with this feather?

*Dicaeopolis.* Is it a feather? what bird's? a braggart's?

*Lamachus.* Hah! I will rip you open.

*Dicaeopolis.* No, no, Lamachus! Violence is out of place here! But as you are so strong, why did you not circumcise me? You have all the tools you need for the operation there.

*Lamachus.* A beggar dares thus address a general!

*Dicaeopolis.* How? Am I a beggar?

*Lamachus.* What are you then?

*Dicaeopolis.* Who am I? A good citizen, not ambitious; a soldier, who has fought well since the outbreak of the war, whereas you are but a vile mercenary.

*Lamachus.* They elected me . . .

*Dicaeopolis.* Yes, three cuckoos did! If I have concluded peace, it was disgust that drove me; for I see men with hoary heads in the ranks and young fellows of your age shirking service. Some are in Thrace getting an allowance of three drachmae, such fellows as Tisamenophaenippus and Panurgipparchides. The others are with Chares or in Chaonia, men like Geretotheodorus and Diomialazon; there are some of the same kidney, too, at Camarina, at Gela, and at Catagela.

*Lamachus.* They were elected.

*Dicaeopolis.* And why do you always receive your pay, when none of these others ever gets any? Speak, Marilades, you have grey hair; well then, have you ever been entrusted with a mission? See! he shakes his head. Yet he is an active as well as a prudent man. And you, Anthracyllus or Euphorides or Prinides, have you knowledge of Ecbatana or Chaonia? You say no, do you not? Such offices are good for the son of Coesyra and Lamachus, who, but yesterday ruined with debt, never pay their shot, and whom all their friends avoid as foot passengers dodge the folks who empty their slops out of window.

*Lamachus.* Oh! in freedom's name! are such exaggerations to be borne?

*Dicaeopolis.* Not unless Lamachus gets paid for it.

*Lamachus.* But I propose always to war with the Peloponnesians, both at sea, on land and everywhere to make them tremble, and trounce them soundly. (*He goes back into his house.*)

*Dicaeopolis.* For my own part, I make proclamation to all Peloponnesians, Megarians and Boeotians, that to them my markets are open; but I debar Lamachus from entering them.

*Leader of the Chorus.* Convinced by this man's speech, the folk have changed their view and approve him for having concluded peace. But let us prepare for the recital of the parabasis. (*The Chorus moves forward and faces the audience.*) Never since our poet presented comedies, has he praised himself upon the stage; but, having been slandered by his enemies amongst the volatile Athenians, accused of scoffing at his country and of insulting the people, to-day he wishes to reply and regain for himself the inconstant Athenians. He maintains that he has done much that is good for you; if you no longer allow yourselves to be too much hoodwinked by strangers or seduced by flattery, if in politics you are no longer the ninnies you once were, it is thanks to him. Formerly, when delegates from other cities wanted to deceive you, they had but to style you, "the people crowned with violets," and at the word "violets" you at once sat erect on the tips of your bums. Or if, to tickle your vanity, someone spoke of "rich and sleek Athens," in return for that "sleekness" he would get anything he wanted, because he spoke of you as he would have of anchovies in oil. In cautioning you against such wiles, the poet has done you great service as well as in forcing you to understand what is really the democratic principle. Thus the strangers, who came to pay their tributes, wanted to see this great poet, who had dared to speak the truth to Athens. And so far has the fame of his boldness reached that one day the Great King, when questioning the Lacedaemonian delegates, first asked them which of the two rival cities was the superior at sea, and then immediately demanded at which it was that the comic poet directed his biting satire. "Happy that city," he added, "if it listens to his counsel; it will grow in power, and its victory is assured." This is why the Lacedaemonians offer you peace, if you will cede them Aegina; not that they care for the isle, but they wish to rob you of your poet. As for you, never lose him, who will always fight for the cause of justice in his comedies; he promises you that his precepts will lead you to happiness, though he uses neither flattery, nor bribery, nor intrigue, nor deceit; instead of loading you with praise, he will point you to the better way. I scoff at Cleon's tricks and plotting; honesty and justice shall fight my cause; never will you find me a political poltroon, a prostitute to the highest bidder.

*First Semi-Chorus.* I invoke thee, Acharnian Muse, fierce and fell as the devouring fire; sudden as the spark that bursts from the crackling oaken coal when roused by the quickening fan to fry little fishes, while others knead the dough or whip the sharp Thasian pickle with rapid hand, so break forth, my Muse, and inspire thy tribesmen with rough, vigorous, stirring strains.

*Leader of First Semi-Chorus.* We others, now old men and heavy with years, we reproach the city; so many are the victories we have gained for the Athenian fleets that we well deserve to be cared for in our declining life; yet far from this, we are ill-used, harassed with law-suits, delivered over to the scorn of stripling orators. Our minds and bodies being ravaged with age, Posidon should protect us, yet we have no other support than a staff. When standing before the judge, we can scarcely stammer forth the fewest words, and of justice we see but its barest shadow, whereas the accuser, desirous of conciliating the younger men, overwhelms us with his ready rhetoric; he drags us before the judge, presses us with questions, lays traps for us; the onslaught troubles, upsets and ruins poor old Tithonus, who, crushed with age, stands tongue-tied; sentenced to a fine, he weeps, he sobs and says to his friend, "This fine robs me of the last trifle that was to have bought my coffin."

*Second Semi-Chorus.* Is this not a scandal? What! the clepsydra is to kill the white-haired veteran, who, in fierce fighting, has so oft covered himself with glorious sweat, whose valour at Marathon saved the country! We were the ones who pursued on the field of Marathon, whereas now it is wretches who pursue us to the death and crush us. What would Marpsias reply to this?

*Leader of Second Semi-Chorus.* What an injustice that a man, bent with age like Thucydides, should be browbeaten by this braggart advocate, Cephisodemus, who is as savage as the Scythian desert he was born in! I wept tears of pity when I saw a Scythian maltreat this old man, who, by Ceres, when he was young and the true Thucydides, would not have permitted an insult from Ceres herself! At that date he would have floored ten orators like Euathlus, he would have terrified three thousand Scythians with his shouts; he would have pierced the whole line of the enemy with his shafts. Ah! but if you will not leave the aged in peace, decree that the advocates be matched; thus the old man will only be confronted with a toothless greybeard, the young will fight with the braggart, the ignoble with the son of Clinias; make a law that in the future, the old man can only be summoned and convicted at the courts by the aged and the young man by the youth.

*Dicaeopolis (coming out of his house and marking out a square in front of it).* These are the confines of my market-place. All Peloponnesians, Megarians, Boeotians, have the right to come and trade here, provided they sell their wares to me and not to Lamachus. As market-inspectors I appoint these three whips of Leprean leather, chosen by lot. Warned away are all informers and all men of Phasis. They are bringing me the pillar on which the treaty is inscribed and I shall erect it in the centre of the market, well in sight of all.

*(He goes back into the house just as a Megarian enters from the left, carrying a sack on his shoulder and followed by his two little daughters.)*

*Megarian.* Hail! market of Athens, beloved of Megarians. Let Zeus, the patron of friendship, witness, I regretted you as a mother mourns her son. Come, poor little daughters of an unfortunate father, try to find something to eat; listen to me with the full heed of an empty belly. Which would you prefer? To be sold or to cry with hunger?

*Daughters.* To be sold, to be sold!

*Megarian.* That is my opinion too. But who would make so sorry a deal as to buy you? Ah! I recall me a Megarian trick; I am going to disguise you as little porkers, that I am offering for sale. Fit your hands with these hoofs and take care to appear the issue of a sow of good breed, for, if I am forced to take you back to the house, by Hermes! you will suffer cruelly of hunger! Then fix on these snouts and cram yourselves into this sack. Forget not to grunt and to say wee-wee like the little pigs that are sacrificed in the Mysteries. I must summon Dicaeopolis. Where is he? Dicaeopolis, do you want to buy some nice little porkers?

*Dicaeopolis (coming out of his house).* Who are you? a Megarian?

*Megarian.* I have come to your market.

*Dicaeopolis.* Well, how are things at Megara?

*Megarian.* We are crying with hunger at our firesides.

*Dicaeopolis.* The fireside is jolly enough with a piper. But what else is doing at Megara?

*Megarian.* What else? When I left for the market, the

authorities were taking steps to let us die in the quickest
manner.

*Dicaeopolis.* That is the best way to get you out of all
your troubles.

*Megarian.* True.

*Dicaeopolis.* What other news of Megara? What is
wheat selling at?

*Megarian.* With us it is valued as highly as the very
gods in heaven!

*Dicaeopolis.* Is it salt that you are bringing?

*Megarian.* Aren't you the ones that are holding back
the salt?

*Dicaeopolis.* Is it garlic then?

*Megarian.* What! garlic! do you not at every raid like
mice grub up the ground with your pikes to pull out
every single head?

*Dicaeopolis.* What *are* you bringing then?

*Megarian.* Little sows, like those they immolate at the
Mysteries.

*Dicaeopolis.* Ah! very well, show me them.

*Megarian.* They are very fine; feel their weight. See!
how fat and fine.

*Dicaeopolis* (*feeling around in the sack*). Hey! what's
this?

*Megarian.* A sow.

*Dicaeopolis.* A *sow*, you say? Where from, then?

*Megarian.* From Megara. What! isn't it a sow then?

*Dicaeopolis* (*feeling around in the sack again*). No, I
don't believe it is.

*Megarian.* This is too much! what an incredulous man!
He says it's not a sow; but we will stake, if you will, a
measure of salt ground up with thyme, that in good
Greek this is called a sow and nothing else.

*Dicaeopolis.* But a sow of the human kind.

*Megarian.* Without question, by Diocles! of my own

breed! Well! What think you? would you like to hear them squeal?

*Dicaeopolis*. Yes, I would.

*Megarian*. Cry quickly, wee sowlet; squeak up, hussy, or by Hermes! I take you back to the house.

*Daughters*. Wee-wee, wee-wee!

*Megarian*. Is that a little sow, or not?

*Dicaeopolis*. Yes, it seems so; but let it grow up, and it will be a fine fat thing.

*Megarian*. In five years it will be just like its mother.

*Dicaeopolis*. But it cannot be sacrificed.

*Megarian*. And why not?

*Dicaeopolis*. It has no tail.

*Megarian*. Because it is quite young, but in good time it will have a big one, thick and red. But if you are willing to bring it up you will have a very fine sow.

*Dicaeopolis*. The two are as like as two peas.

*Megarian*. They are born of the same father and mother; let them be fattened, let them grow their bristles, and they will be the finest sows you can offer to Aphrodité.

*Dicaeopolis*. But sows are not immolated to Aphrodité.

*Megarian*. Not sows to Aphrodité! Why, she's the only goddess to whom they are offered! The flesh of my sows will be excellent on your spit.

*Dicaeopolis*. Can they eat alone? They no longer need their mother?

*Megarian*. Certanly not, nor their father.

*Dicaeopolis*. What do they like most?

*Megarian*. Whatever is given them; but ask for yourself.

*Dicaeopolis*. Speak! little sow.

*Daughters*. Wee-wee, wee-wee!

*Dicaeopolis*. Can you eat chick-pease?

*Daughters*. Wee-wee, wee-wee, wee-wee!

*Dicaeopolis.* And Attic figs?

*Daughters.* Wee-wee, wee-wee!

*Dicaeopolis.* What sharp squeaks at the name of figs. Come, let some figs be brought for these little pigs. Will they eat them? Goodness! how they munch them, what a grinding of teeth, mighty Heracles! I believe those pigs hail from the land of the Voracians.

*Megarian.* But they have not eaten all the figs; I took this one myself.

*Dicaeopolis.* Ah! what curious creatures! For what sum will you sell them?

*Megarian.* I will give you one for a bunch of garlic, and the other, if you like, for a quart measure of salt.

*Dicaeopolis.* I'll buy them. Wait for me here. (*He goes into the house.*)

*Megarian.* The deal is done. Hermes, god of good traders, grant I may sell both my wife and my mother in the same way!

(*An Informer enters.*)

*Informer.* Hi! fellow, what country are you from?

*Megarian.* I am a pig-merchant from Megara.

*Informer.* I shall denounce both your pigs and yourself as public enemies.

*Megarian.* Ah! here our troubles begin afresh!

*Informer.* Let go of that sack. I'll teach you to talk Megarian!

*Megarian.* Dicaeopolis, Dicaeopolis, they want to denounce me.

*Dicaeopolis* (*from within*). Who dares do this thing? (*He comes out of his house.*) Inspectors, drive out the informers. Ah! you offer to enlighten us without a lamp!

*Informer.* What! I may not denounce our enemies?

*Dicaeopolis* (*with a threatening gesture*). Watch out

for yourself, and go off pretty quick and denounce else-where.

(*The Informer runs away.*)

*Megarian.* What a plague to Athens!

*Dicaeopolis.* Be reassured, Megarian. Here is the price for your two sowlets, the garlic and the salt. Farewell and much happiness!

*Megarian.* Ah! we never have that amongst us.

*Dicaeopolis.* Oh, I'm sorry if I said the wrong thing.

*Megarian.* Farewell, dear little sows, and seek, far from your father, to munch your bread with salt, if they give you any.

*Chorus.* Here is a man truly happy. See how every-thing succeeds to his wish. Peacefully seated in his market, he will earn his living; woe to Ctesias, and all other informers who dare to enter there! You will not be cheated as to the value of wares, you will not again see Prepis wiping his big arse, nor will Cleony-mus jostle you; you will take your walks, clothed in a fine tunic, without meeting Hyperbolus and his unceasing quibblings, without being accosted on the public place by any importunate fellow, neither by Cratinus, shaven in the fashion of the adulterers, nor by this musician, who plagues us with his silly improvisations, that hyper-rogue Artemo, with his arm-pits stinking as foul as a goat, like his father be-fore him. You will not be the butt of the villainous Pauson's jeers, nor of Lysistratus, the disgrace of the Cholargian deme, who is the incarnation of all the vices, and endures cold and hunger more than thirty days in the month.

# THE ACHARNIANS

*(A Boeotian enters, followed by his slave, who is carrying a large assortment of articles of food, and by a troop of flute players.)*

*Boeotian.* By Heracles! my shoulder is quite black and blue. Ismenias, put the penny-royal down there very gently, and all of you, musicians from Thebes, strike up on your bone flutes "The Dog's Arse."

*(The Musicians immediately begin an atrocious rendition of a vulgar tune.)*

*Dicaeopolis.* Enough, damn you; get out of here! Rascally hornets, away with you! Whence has sprung this accursed swarm of Chaeris fellows which comes assailing my door?

*(The Musicians depart.)*

*Boeotian.* Ah! by Iolas! Drive them off, my dear host, you will please me immensely; all the way from Thebes, they were there piping behind me and they have completely stripped my penny-royal of its blossom. But will you buy anything of me, some chickens or some locusts?

*Dicaeopolis.* Ah! good day, Boeotian, eater of good round loaves. What do *you* bring?

*Boeotian.* All that is good in Boeotia, marjoram, penny-royal, rush-mats, lamp-wicks, ducks, jays, woodcocks, water-fowl, wrens, divers.

*Dicaeopolis.* A regular hail of birds is beating down on my market.

*Boeotian.* I also bring geese, hares, foxes, moles, hedgehogs, cats, lyres, martins, otters and eels from the Copaic lake.

*Dicaeopolis.* Ah! my friend, you, who bring me the most delicious of fish, let me salute your eels.

# ARISTOPHANES

*Boeotian.* Come, thou, the eldest of my fifty Copaic virgins, come and complete the joy of our host.

*Dicaeopolis* (*likewise*). Oh! my well-beloved, thou object of my long regrets, thou art here at last then, thou, after whom the comic poets sigh, thou, who are dear to Morychus. Slaves, hither with the stove and the bellows. Look at this charming eel, that returns to us after six long years of absence. Salute it, my children; as for myself, I will supply coal to do honour to the stranger. Take it into my house; death itself could not separate me from her, if cooked with beet leaves.

*Boeotian.* And what will you give me in return?

*Dicaeopolis.* It will pay for your market dues. And as to the rest, what do you wish to sell me?

*Boeotian.* Why, everything.

*Dicaeopolis.* On what terms? For ready-money or in wares from these parts?

*Boeotian.* I would take some Athenian produce, that we have not got in Boeotia.

*Dicaeopolis.* Phaleric anchovies, pottery?

*Boeotian.* Anchovies, pottery? But these we have. I want produce that is wanting with us and that is plentiful here.

*Dicaeopolis.* Ah! I have the very thing; take away an informer, packed up carefully as crockery-ware.

*Boeotian.* By the twin gods! I should earn big money, if I took one; I would exhibit him as an ape full of spite.

*Dicaeopolis* (*as an informer enters*). Hah! here we have Nicarchus, who comes to denounce you.

*Boeotian.* How small he is!

*Dicaeopolis.* But all pure evil.

*Nicarchus.* Whose are these goods?

*Dicaeopolis.* Mine; they come from Boeotia, I call Zeus to witness.

*Nicarchus.* I denounce them as coming from an enemy's country.

*Boeotian.* What! you declare war against birds?

*Nicarchus.* And I am going to denounce you too.

*Boeotian.* What harm have I done you?

*Nicarchus.* I will say it for the benefit of those that listen; you introduce lamp-wicks from an enemy's country.

*Dicaeopolis.* Then you even denounce a wick.

*Nicarchus.* It needs but one to set an arsenal afire.

*Dicaeopolis.* A wick set an arsenal ablaze! But how, great gods?

*Nicarchus.* Should a Boeotian attach it to an insect's wing, and, taking advantage of a violent north wind, throw it by means of a tube into the arsenal and the fire once get hold of the vessels, everything would soon be devoured by the flames.

*Dicaeopolis.* Ah! wretch! an insect and a wick devour everything! (*He strikes him.*)

*Nicarchus* (*to the Chorus*). You will bear witness, that he mishandles me.

*Dicaeopolis* (*to the Boeotian*). Shut his mouth. Give me some hay; I am going to pack him up like a vase, that he may not get broken on the road.

(*The Informer is bound and gagged and packed in hay.*)

*Leader of the Chorus.* Pack up your goods carefully, friend; that the stranger may not break it when taking it away.

*Dicaeopolis.* I shall take great care with it. (*He hits the Informer on the head and a stifled cry is heard.*) One would say he is cracked already; he rings with a false note, which the gods abhor.

*Leader of the Chorus.* But what will be done with him?

*Dicaeopolis.* This is a vase good for all purposes; it

will be used as a vessel for holding all foul things, a mortar for pounding together law-suits, a lamp for spying upon accounts, and as a cup for the mixing up and poisoning of everything.

*Leader of the Chorus.* None could ever trust a vessel for domestic use that has such a ring about it.

*Dicaeopolis.* Oh! it is strong, my friend, and will never get broken, if care is taken to hang it head downwards.

*Leader of the Chorus.* There! it is well packed now!

*Boeotian.* Well then, I will proceed to carry off my bundle.

*Leader of the Chorus.* Farewell, worthiest of strangers, take this informer, good for anything, and fling him where you like.

*Dicaeopolis.* Bah! this rogue has given me enough trouble to pack! Here! Boeotian, pick up your pottery.

*Boeotian.* Stoop, Ismenias, that I may put it on your shoulder, and be very careful with it.

*Dicaeopolis.* You carry nothing worth having; however, take it, for you will profit by your bargain; the informers will bring you luck.

(*The Boeotian and his slave depart; Dicaeopolis goes into his house; a slave comes out of Lamachus' house.*)

*Slave.* Dicaeopolis!

*Dicaeopolis.* What's the matter? Why are you calling me?

*Slave.* Lamachus wants to keep the Feast of Cups, and I come by his order to bid you one drachma for some thrushes and three more for a Copaic eel.

*Dicaeopolis* (*coming out*). And who is this Lamachus, who demands an eel?

*Slave.* He is the terrible, indefatigable Lamachus, who is always brandishing his fearful Gorgon's head and the three plumes which o'ershadow his helmet.

*Dicaeopolis.* No, no, he will get nothing, even though he gave me his buckler. Let him eat salt fish while he shakes his plumes, and, if he comes here making any din, I shall call the inspectors. As for myself, I shall take away all these goods; (*in tragic style*) I go home on thrushes' wings and blackbirds' pinions. (*He goes into his house.*)

*First Semi-Chorus.* You see, citizens, you see the good fortune which this man owes to his prudence, to his profound wisdom. You see how, since he has concluded peace, he buys what is useful in the household and good to eat hot. All good things flow towards him unsought. Never will I welcome the god of war in *my* house; never shall *he* sing the "Harmodius" at my table; he is a sot, who comes feasting with those who are overflowing with good things and brings all manner of mischief in his train. He overthrows, ruins, rips open; it is vain to make him a thousand offers, to say "be seated, pray, and drink this cup, proffered in all friendship"; he burns our vine-stocks and brutally spills on the ground the wine from our vineyards.

*Second Semi-Chorus.* This man, on the other hand, covers his table with a thousand dishes; proud of his good fortunes, he has had these feathers cast before his door to show us how he lives. (*A woman appears, bearing the attributes of Peace.*) Oh, Peace! companion of fair Aphrodité and of the sweet Graces, how charming are thy features and yet I never knew it! Would that Eros might join me to thee, Eros crowned with roses as Zeuxis shows him to us! Do I seem somewhat old to thee? I am yet able to make thee a threefold offering; despite my age I could plant a long row of vines for you; then beside these some tender cuttings from the fig; finally a young vine-stock, loaded with fruit, and all around the field olive trees, to furnish us with oil wherewith to anoint us both at the New Moons.

(*A Herald enters.*)

*Herald.* Oyez, oyez! As was the custom of your forebears, empty a full pitcher of wine at the call of the trumpet; he who first sees the bottom shall get a wineskin as round and plump as Ctesiphon's belly.

*Dicaeopolis* (*coming out of the house; to his family within*). Women, children, have you not heard? Faith! do you not heed the herald? Quick! let the hares boil and roast merrily; keep them turning; withdraw them from the flame; prepare the chaplets; reach me the skewers that I may spit the thrushes.

*Leader of First Semi-Chorus.* I envy you your wisdom and even more your good cheer.

*Dicaeopolis.* What then will you say when you see the thrushes roasting?

*Leader of First Semi-Chorus.* Ah! true indeed!

*Dicaeopolis.* Slave! stir up the fire.

*Leader of First Semi-Chorus.* See, how he knows his business, what a perfect cook! How well he understands the way to prepare a good dinner!

(*A Husbandman enters in haste.*)

*Husbandman.* Ah! woe is me!

*Dicaeopolis.* Heracles! What have we here?

*Husbandman.* A most miserable man.

*Dicaeopolis.* Keep your misery for yourself.

*Husbandman.* Ah! friend! since you alone are enjoying peace, grant me a part of your truce, were it but five years.

*Dicaeopolis.* What has happened to you?

*Husbandman.* I am ruined; I have lost a pair of steers.

*Dicaeopolis.* How?

*Husbandman.* The Boeotians seized them at Phylé.

*Dicaeopolis.* Ah! poor wretch! and do you still wear white?

*Husbandman.* Their dung made my wealth.

*Dicaeopolis.* What can I do in the matter?

*Husbandman.* Crying for my beasts has lost me my eyesight. Ah! if you care for poor Dercetes of Phylé, anoint mine eyes quickly with your balm of peace.

*Dicaeopolis.* But, my poor fellow, I do not practise medicine.

*Husbandman.* Come, I adjure you; perhaps I shall recover my steers.

*Dicaeopolis.* Impossible; away, go and whine to the disciples of Pittalus.

*Husbandman.* Grant me but one drop of peace; pour it into this little reed.

*Dicaeopolis.* No, not a particle; go and weep somewhere else.

*Husbandman.* Oh! oh! oh! my poor beasts!

*Leader of Second Semi-Chorus.* This man has discovered the sweetest enjoyment in peace; he will share it with none.

*Dicaeopolis (to a slave).* Pour honey over this tripe; set it before the fire to dry.

*Leader of Second Semi-Chorus.* What lofty tones he uses! Did you hear him?

*Dicaeopolis (to the slaves inside the house).* Get the eels on the gridiron!

*Leader of Second Semi-Chorus.* You are killing me with hunger; your smoke is choking your neighbours, and you split our ears with your bawling.

*Dicaeopolis.* Have this fried and let it be nicely browned.

*(He goes back into the house. A Wedding Guest enters, carrying a package.)*

**Wedding Guest.** Dicaeopolis! Dicaeopolis!

*Dicaeopolis.* Who are you?

**Wedding Guest.** A young bridegroom sends you these viands from the marriage feast.

*Dicaeopolis.* Whoever he be, I thank him.

**Wedding Guest.** And in return, he prays you to pour a glass of peace into this vase, that he may not have to go to the front and may stay at home to make love to his young wife.

*Dicaeopolis.* Take back, take back your viands; for a thousand drachmae I would not give a drop of peace. *(A young woman enters.)* But who is she?

**Wedding Guest.** She is the matron of honour; she wants to say something to you from the bride privately.

*Dicaeopolis.* Come, what do you wish to say? *(The Matron of Honour whispers in his ear.)* Ah! what a ridiculous demand! The bride burns with longing to keep her husband's tool at home. Come! bring hither my truce; to her alone will I give some of it, for she is a woman, and, as such, should not suffer under the war. Here, friend, hand me your vial. And as to the manner of applying this balm, tell the bride, when a levy of soldiers is made, to rub some in bed on her husband, where most needed. *(The Matron of Honour and the Wedding Guest depart.)* There, slave, take away my truce! Now, quick, bring me the wine-flagon, that I may fill up the drinking bowls!

*(The slave leaves. A Herald enters.)*

*Leader of the Chorus.* I see a man, "striding along space, with knitted brows; he seems to us the bearer of terrible tidings."

*Herald.* Oh! toils and battles and Lamachuses! (*He knocks on Lamachus' door.*)

*Lamachus.* What noise resounds around my dwelling, where shines the glint of arms.

*Herald.* The Generals order you forthwith to take your battalions and your plumes, and, despite the snow, to go and guard our borders. They have learnt that a band of Boeotians intend taking advantage of the Feast of Cups to invade our country.

*Lamachus.* Ah! the Generals! they are numerous, but not good for much! It's cruel, not to be able to enjoy the feast!

*Dicaeopolis.* Oh! warlike host of Lamachus!

*Lamachus.* Wretch! do you dare to jeer me?

*Dicaeopolis.* Do you want to fight this four-winged Geryon?

*Lamachus.* Oh! oh! what fearful tidings!

*Dicaeopolis.* Ah! ah! I see another herald running up; what news does he bring me?

(*Another Herald enters.*)

*Herald.* Dicaeopolis!

*Dicaeopolis.* What is the matter?

*Herald.* Come quickly to the feast and bring your basket and your cup; it is the priest of Bacchus who invites you. But hasten, the guests have been waiting for you a long while. All is ready—couches, tables, cushions, chaplets, perfumes, dainties and whores to boot; biscuits, cakes, sesamé-bread, tarts, lovely dancing women, and the "Harmodius." But come with all speed.

*Lamachus.* Oh! hostile gods!

*Dicaeopolis.* This is not astounding; you have chosen this great ugly Gorgon's head for your patron. (*to a slave.*) You, shut the door, and let someone get ready the meal.

*Lamachus.* Slave! slave! my knapsack!

*Dicaeopolis.* Slave! slave! a basket!

*Lamachus.* Take salt and thyme, slave, and don't forget the onions.

*Dicaeopolis.* Get some fish for me; I cannot bear onions.

*Lamachus.* Slave, wrap me up a little stale salt meat in a fig-leaf.

*Dicaeopolis.* And for me some nice fat tripe in a fig-leaf; I will have it cooked here.

*Lamachus.* Bring me the plumes for my helmet.

*Dicaeopolis.* Bring me wild pigeons and thrushes.

*Lamachus.* How white and beautiful are these ostrich feathers!

*Dicaeopolis.* How fat and well browned is the flesh of this wood-pigeon!

*Lamachus.* My friend, stop scoffing at my armour.

*Dicaeopolis.* My friend, stop staring at my thrushes.

*Lamachus (to his slave).* Bring me the case for my triple plume.

*Dicaepolis (to his slave).* Pass me over that dish of hare.

*Lamachus.* Alas! the moths have eaten the hair of my crest.

*Dicaeopolis.* Shall I eat my hare before dinner?

*Lamachus.* My friend, will you kindly not speak to me?

*Dicaeopolis.* I'm not speaking to you; I'm scolding my slave. *(to the slave.)* Shall we wager and submit the matter to Lamachus, which of the two is the best to eat, a locust or a thrush?

*Lamachus.* Insolent hound!

*Dicaeopolis.* He much prefers the locusts.

*Lamachus.* Slave, unhook my spear and bring it to me.

*Dicaepolis.* Slave, slave, take the sausage from the fire and bring it to me.

*Lamachus.* Come, let me draw my spear from its sheath. Hold it, slave, hold it tight.

*Dicaeopolis.* And you, slave, grip well hold of the skewer.

*Lamachus.* Slave, the bracings for my shield.

*Dicaeopolis.* Pull the loaves out of the oven and bring me these bracings of my stomach.

*Lamachus.* My round buckler with the Gorgon's head.

*Dicaeopolis.* My round cheese-cake.

*Lamachus.* What clumsy wit!

*Dicaeopolis.* What delicious cheese-cake!

*Lamachus.* Pour oil on the buckler. Hah! hah! I can see reflected there an old man who will be accused of cowardice.

*Dicaeopolis.* Pour honey on the cake. Hah! hah! I can see an old man who makes Lamachus of the Gorgon's head weep with rage.

*Lamachus.* Slave, full war armour.

*Dicaeopolis.* Slave, my beaker; that is *my* armour.

*Lamachus.* With this I hold my ground with any foe.

*Dicaeopolis.* And I with this in any drinking bout.

*Lamachus.* Fasten the strappings to the buckler.

*Dicaeopolis.* Pack the dinner well into the basket.

*Lamachus.* Personally I shall carry the knapsack.

*Dicaeopolis.* Personally I shall carry the cloak.

*Lamachus.* Slave, take up the buckler and let's be off. It is snowing! God help us! A wintry business!

*Dicaeopolis.* Take up the basket, mine's a festive business.

(*They depart in opposite directions.*)

*Leader of the Chorus.* We wish you both joy on your journeys, which differ so much. One goes to mount guard and freeze, while the other will drink, crowned with flowers, and then lie with a young beauty.

*Chorus* (*singing*). I say it freely; may Zeus confound Antimachus, the poet-historian, the son of Psacas! When Choregus at the Lenaea, alas! alas! he dismissed me dinnerless. May I see him devouring with his eyes a cuttle-fish, just served, well cooked, hot and properly salted; and the moment that he stretches his hand to help himself, may a dog seize it and run off with it. Such is my first wish. I also hope for him a misfortune at night. That returning all-fevered from horse practise, he may meet an Orestes, mad with drink, who will crack him over the head; that wishing to seize a stone, he, in the dark, may pick up a fresh turd, hurl, miss him and hit Cratinus.

*(The slave of Lamachus enters.)*

*Slave of Lamachus* (*knocking on the door of Lamachus' house*). Captives present within the house of Lamachus, water, water in a little pot! Make it warm, get ready cloths, cerate, greasy wool and bandages for his ankle. In leaping a ditch, the master has hurt himself against a stake; he has dislocated and twisted his ankle, broken his head by falling on a stone, while his Gorgon shot far away from his buckler. His mighty braggadocio plume rolled on the ground; at this sight he uttered these doleful words, "Radiant star, I gaze on thee for the last time; my eyes close to all light, I die." Having said this, he falls into the water, gets out again, meets some runaways and pursues the robbers with his spear at their backsides. But here he comes, himself. Get the door open.

*Lamachus* (*limping in with the help of two soldiers and singing a song of woe*). Oh! heavens; oh; heavens! What cruel pain! I faint, I tremble! Alas! I die! the foe's lance has struck me! But what would hurt me most would be for Dicaeopolis to see me wounded thus and laugh at my ill-fortune.

*Dicaeopolis* (*enters with two courtesans, singing gaily*). Oh! my gods! what breasts! Swelling like quinces! Come, my treasures, give me voluptuous kisses! Glue your lips to mine. Haha! I was the first to empty my cup.

*Lamachus*. Oh! cruel fate! how I suffer! accursed wounds!

*Dicaeopolis*. Hah! hah! Hail! Lamachippus!

*Lamachus*. Woe is me!

*Dicaeopolis* (*to the one girl*). Why do you kiss me?

*Lamachus*. Ah, wretched me!

*Dicaeopolis* (*to the other girl*). And why do you bite me?

*Lamachus*. 'Twas a cruel score I was paying back!

*Dicaeopolis*. Scores are not evened at the Feast of Cups!

*Lamachus*. Oh! Oh! Paean, Paean!

*Dicaeopolis*. But to-day is not the feast of Paean.

*Lamachus* (*to the soldiers*). Oh! take hold of my leg, do; ah! hold it tenderly, my friends!

*Dicaeopolis* (*to the girls*). And you, my darlings, embrace me, both of you!

*Lamachus*. This blow with the stone makes me dizzy; my sight grows dim.

*Dicaeopolis*. For myself, I want to get to bed and to make love in the dark.

*Lamachus*. Carry me to the surgeon Pittalus. Put me in his healing hands!

*Dicaeopolis*. Take me to the judges. Where is the king of the feast? The wine-skin is mine!

*Lamachus* (*as he is being carried away*). That spear has pierced my bones; what torture I endure!

*Dicaeopolis* (*to the audience*). You see this empty cup! I triumph! I triumph!

*Chorus.* Old man, I come at your bidding! You triumph! you triumph!

*Dicaeopolis.* Again I have brimmed my cup with unmixed wine and drained it at a draught!

*Chorus.* You triumph then, brave champion; thine is the wine-skin!

*Dicaeopolis.* Follow me, singing "Triumph! Triumph!"

*Chorus.* Aye! we will sing of thee, thee and thy sacred wine-skin, and we all, as we follow thee, will repeat in thine honour, "Triumph, Triumph!"

## AIRMONT CLASSICS